SCHOLASTIC

The BIG BOOK of Reading Response Activities

by Michael Gravois

New York · Toronto · London · Auckland · Sydney
Mexico City · New Delhi · Hong Kong · Buenos Aires

Teaching *Resources*

Dedication

To the newest additions—

Durham Michael Gravois,
Mackenzie Lynne Lund,
and Amelia Cecilia McGrath

Cover design by Lillian Kohli and Jason Robinson
Interior design by Michael Gravois
Illustrations by Dave Clegg (except for pages 48–50 by Jim Palmer)

ISBN-13: 978-0-439-79683-5
ISBN-10: 0-439-79683-0

CONTENTS

Postreading Activities

Introduction

Creating a book-rich environment is the first step toward developing a literate classroom community where children learn to read and read to learn. *The Big Book of Reading Response Activities* is designed to help you cultivate a classroom filled with willing readers by providing you with scores of hands-on activities, projects, bulletin boards, and creative dramatic ideas that are sure to get your students excited about reading, talking about reading, and writing about reading. The flexibility of these activities addresses the different intelligences found within every classroom by allowing students the freedom to use their individual strengths to find connections between the text and their own lives. The easy-to-make projects will encourage students to develop techniques for expressing their ideas visually; the creative dramatics activities will get students up and out of their seats and kinesthetically involved in their responses to reading; and the graphic organizers will help students organize their thoughts as they reflect on what they've read.

Using This Book

This book is divided into three main sections—prereading activities, reading activities, and postreading activities. Certainly, many of the activities can be shifted to another category or adapted to meet your needs. So look through the book and explore the possibilities.

Prereading activities prepare students for the thoughtful process involved in reading. These activities are designed to teach students about the nature of reading and the parts of a book, and they are meant to help develop important reading skills–such as prediction, learning new vocabulary, and identifying major story elements.

Reading activities develop students' awareness of essential practices that proficient readers use—examining character relationships, comprehending the main idea of a passage, and connecting themes from a book to their own life experiences.

Postreading activities require students to reflect on the literature and nonfiction texts they have read. They ask students to recall information from the readings, offer opinions about what they read, and celebrate their accomplishments.

Teacher Tip

Remember to consider your students' interests when planning your reading lessons and choosing the books you're going to use. Selecting books that appeal to students— both in content and in theme—can ensure that you will soon have a class of avid readers.

Leveling Tip

Spend time in your local and school libraries to learn about the quality children's books that are available. This will help you recommend books that match students' interests and reading levels.

Book Talk

"Reading, in contrast to sitting before the screen, is not a purely passive exercise. The child, particularly one who reads a book dealing with real life, has nothing before it but the hieroglyphics of the printed page. Imagination must do the rest; and imagination is called upon to do it. Not so the television screen. Here everything is spelled out for the viewer, visually, in motion, and in all three dimensions. No effort of imagination is called upon for its enjoyment."
–George F. Kennan (1993)

Check the little bookworm on the title page of each activity to learn the skill being taught and the type of activity it is. There are four major types of activities in this book:

The Skill Is Listed Here
- Type of Activity -
Fiction/Nonfiction

- **Activities:** These are hands-on projects that ask students to create a manipulative of some sort or encourage them to interact with one another and discuss aspects of reading.

- **Graphic Organizers:** Graphic organizers help students organize their thoughts as they respond to their reading. Templates are provided for you to copy and pass out to the class.

- **Bulletin Boards:** These activities help you create an environment that gives the students ownership of their space by surrounding them with examples of their work.

- **Creative Dramatics:** In its simplest form, creative dramatics is structured play. In its truest form, creative dramatics promotes social skills, literacy skills, confidence, independent thought, and problem-solving skills. And it is sure to fill your classroom with laughter.

The icons used in the sidebars of this book offer tips and advice related to each activity

Teacher Tip–These tips suggest extensions and alternate uses for the activities.

Leveling Tip–These pointers provide ideas for adapting the activities to a range of learning levels and abilities.

Cross-Curriculum–These sidebars present ways in which the activities can be used in other subject areas.

Book Talk–Read what the experts have to say about different reading skills and strategies.

Connections to the Language Arts Standards

The activities in this book help students meet the language arts standards outlined by Mid-continent Research for Education and Learning (www.mcrel.org), a nationally recognized nonprofit organization that collects and synthesizes national and state K–12 standards.

Uses the general skills and strategies of the writing process

- Uses a variety of strategies to plan research (e.g., identifies possible topic by brainstorming, listing questions, using idea webs; organizes prior knowledge about a topic; develops a course of action; determines how to locate necessary information)
- Writes in response to literature (e.g., summarizes main ideas and significant details; relates own ideas to supporting details; advances judgments; supports judgments with references to the text, other works, other authors, nonprint media, and personal knowledge)

Uses the general skills and strategies of the reading process

- Establishes a purpose for reading (e.g., for information, for pleasure, to understand a specific viewpoint)
- Makes, confirms, and revises simple predictions about what will be found in a text (e.g., uses prior knowledge and ideas presented in text, illustrations, titles, topic sentences, key words, and foreshadowing clues)

Uses reading skills and strategies to understand and interpret a variety of literary texts

- Uses reading skills and strategies to understand a variety of literary passages and texts (e.g., fairy tales, folktales, fiction, nonfiction, myths, poems, fables, fantasies, historical fiction, biographies, autobiographies, chapter books)
- Understands the basic concept of plot (e.g., main problem, conflict, resolution, cause-and-effect)
- Understands elements of character development in literary works (e.g., differences between main and minor characters; stereotypical characters as opposed to fully developed characters; changes that characters undergo; the importance of a character's actions, motives, and appearance to plot and theme)
- Makes connections between characters or simple events in a literary work and people or events in his or her own life

Uses reading skills and strategies to understand and interpret a variety of informational texts

- Understands the main idea and supporting details of simple expository information
- Uses the various parts of a book (e.g., index, table of contents, glossary, appendix, preface) to locate information
- Summarizes and paraphrases information in texts (e.g., includes the main idea and significant supporting details of a reading selection)

Uses listening and speaking strategies for different purposes

- Makes contributions in class and group discussions (e.g., reports on ideas and personal knowledge about a topic, initiates conversations, connects ideas and experiences with those of others)
- Recites and responds to familiar stories, poems, and rhymes with patterns (e.g., relates information to own life; describes character, setting, plot)
- Listens for specific information in spoken texts (e.g., plot details or information about a character in a short story read aloud, information about a familiar topic from a radio broadcast)

Kendall, J. S., & Marzano, R. J. (2004). *Content knowledge: A compendium of standards and benchmarks for K–12 education*. Aurora, CO: Mid-continent Research for Education and Learning.

Read-Around Reports

Materials

- 8- by 30-inch white bulletin board paper
- colored markers and pencils
- rulers
- tape
- hole punch
- scissors
- four 12-inch pieces of string

Purpose

Students create a three-dimensional report and give an oral presentation that highlights aspects of their favorite book.

Directions

1. Give each student an 8- by 30-inch sheet of white bulletin board paper.

2. On the left side of the paper, have students draw a picture that is representative of a scene from their favorite book.

3. Invite students to use creative lettering to write the title of the book, the author's name, and their name across the top of the right side of the paper.

4. Have students include the following below the title:

- a picture of the main character from the book
- a list of other characters from the book
- a few sentences describing things the student liked about the book

Leveling Tip

There is a lot of room for students to respond on a read-around report. Vary the type of information you'd like students to include so it matches their ability level—adjectives describing the setting, word webs about the genre, sentences explaining the main problem and solution, or a timeline of events.

5. Encourage students to use a ruler to neatly organize and lay out the information below the title. They can draw writing lines in pencil, write the text in ink, and then erase the pencil marks.

6. After students have finished writing their reports, have them curl the paper into a cylinder and tape it.

7. Show students how to punch four holes in the top of the report, tie a 12-inch piece of string to each of the holes, and connect the strings to a central string.

8. Invite students to give a short oral report about their book. Encourage them to describe the things they like about it and share information they included on their read-around report.

9. Hang the reports from the ceiling so they are able to spin freely in the breeze.

Cross-Curriculum

Read-around reports are easy to adapt to any curricular need. Students can create nonfiction reports that focus on historical events, famous people, scientific discoveries, or cultures.

Encouraging Reading
- Activity -
Fiction/Nonfiction

Book Links

BOOK LINKS

Book Title: _All The Colors of the Earth_ Date Finished: _March 25_

Author: _Sheila Hamanaka_ Parent: _Mrs. Janice Pearson_

Student: _Meredith_

Materials

- BOOK LINKS template (page 11)
- scissors
- tape

Purpose

Students record books that they've read at home on a paper chain.

Directions

1. Copy the BOOK LINKS template onto sheets of brightly colored paper. Give each student a few copies.

2. Whenever students finish reading a book at home, have them fill out the information on the book link, cut it out, have it signed by a parent or caregiver, and bring it back to class.

3. Encourage students to give a short talk about their book. After the book talk, fold the link into a loop and add it to a class chain of book links.

4. When the chain is long enough to reach across the classroom, celebrate by having a class party. Leave the links up throughout the year so that the class can see how many books they have read.

Teacher Tip

Ask parents or caregivers to discuss each book with their child whenever they sign a book link. Discussing books is one way to foster an excitement for reading. Explain to families that this is not a race to see which child can read more books, but rather a group project to celebrate reading.

Book Links Template

BOOKS LINKS

Book Title: _____

Author: _____

Student: _____

Date Finished: _____

Parent: _____

BOOK LINKS

Book Title: _____

Author: _____

Student: _____

Date Finished: _____

Parent: _____

Mark It!

Making a Bookmark
- Activity -
Fiction/Nonfiction

Purpose

Students create personalized bookmarks.

Directions

1. Pass out half of a copy of the MARK IT! bookmark template to each student.

2. Invite students to use colored pencils to decorate their bookmark. Have them draw a picture in the circle that illustrates a character or scene from a book they are about to read, an icon of a book's cover, a slogan about reading, and so on. Have students write their names below the circle using fancy lettering.

3. Have students cut out the bookmark and write a sentence or two about the importance of reading on the back of the bookmark.

4. Collect and laminate the bookmarks.

5. Use a craft knife to cut along the curved dotted line.

6. Students can slip the bookmark into their books, clipping the tab over the page to mark their place.

Teacher Tip

Students can create bookmarks related to a genre they're studying. For example, a science fiction bookmark might feature an alien saying, "Reading is out of this world!" For a mystery bookmark, students can create a magnifying glass out of the upper circle and write the saying, "Reading is the solution!"

Mark It! Bookmark Templates

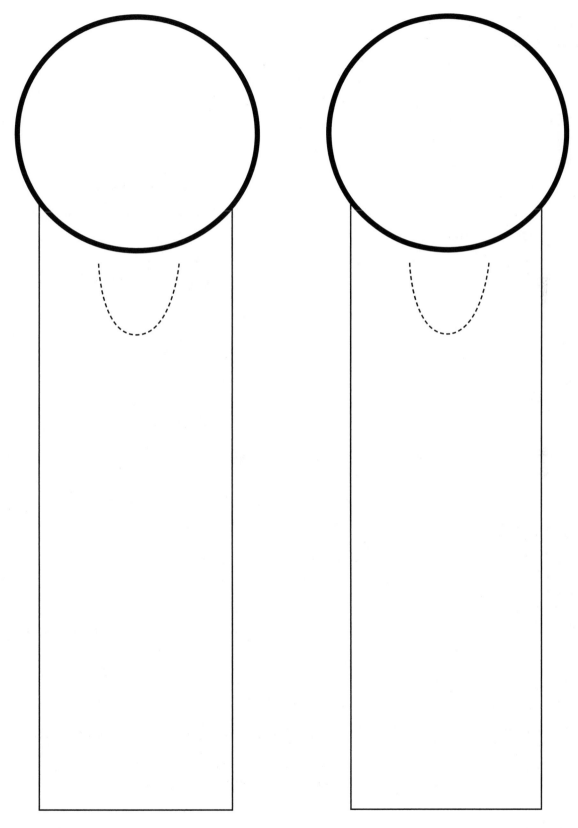

Printmaking

Materials

- clean styrofoam trays
- scissors
- glue
- cardboard
- tape
- water-based block printing ink (or tempera paint)
- metal tray
- rubber brayer
- newsprint
- wooden spoon

Purpose

Students learn about the function of the printing press, how it works, and its importance in the history of reading.

Directions

1. Precut a few dozen two-inch square sections from styrofoam trays.

2. Give each student one square.

3. Assign each student a different letter of the alphabet.

4. Have students cut ¼-inch-wide strips of varying lengths from other styrofoam trays. Show students how to glue the strips onto the two-inch squares of styrofoam in the form of a backward letter to create a print block of the letter. (The print blocks have to show a mirror image of the desired letter because it will print in reverse.)

Cross-Curriculum

Discuss the life of the historical figure Johannes Gutenberg, the inventor of the printing press, with your class. Ask students why the printing press is one of the most important inventions of all time.

5. Have each student create a mirror-image print block of his or her assigned letter. Allow the glue to dry overnight.

6. Collect the print block letters and use them to spell students' names.

7. Place the letters on a sheet of cardboard and tape the edges down so they don't move. (Make sure you spell the names backward so the letters appear in the correct order on the page.)

8. Squirt some water-based block printing ink (or tempera paint) into a metal tray and roll a rubber brayer over it.

9. Roll the brayer over the styrofoam letters to transfer the ink onto the letters.

10. Place a sheet of newsprint over the letters. Rub a large wooden spoon over the surface of the letters. This ensures that the paper touches the entire surface of each letter.

11. Remove the newsprint to reveal the name.

12. Discuss the printmaking process with your students, explaining how similar steps are taken—but on a much larger scale—to print the books and newspapers that people read. Tell students that prior to the invention of the printing press, books had to be written by hand. This made books very rare and expensive. It also made it difficult for people to learn how to read. Ask students if they can tell you how the invention of the printing press affected the spread of news and the education of people.

Johannes Gutenberg

Johannes Gutenberg (ca. 1400–1468) invented the printing press and was a pioneer in the use of movable type. He created small blocks, each with a single letter on its face, which he used to print books. Prior to the invention of the printing press, each book had to be handwritten, a laborious task that could take many years. After this invention, multiple copies of books could be printed. This invention greatly improved communication, literacy, and the flow of ideas. It helped usher in the age of enlightenment and the Renaissance.

Parts
of a Book
- Activity -
Nonfiction

The Sum of Its Parts

Answers to Quiz

1. body

2. dedication

3. cover

4. glossary

5. table of contents

6. illustrator

7. index

8. author

Purpose

Students identify the various parts of a book and learn how to use them to locate information.

Directions

1. Review the PARTS OF A BOOK reproducible with students.

2. Use a sample book or textbook to illustrate the different parts of a book.

3. Pass out the PARTS OF A BOOK quiz to assess students' understanding.

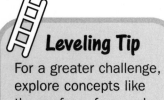

Leveling Tip

For a greater challenge, explore concepts like the preface, foreword, introduction, and bibliography of a book.

Name Alison   Date January 10

Parts of a Book Quiz
Use the word bank to answer each of these questions.

1. The part of a book that contains the most words
   body
2. The part of a book where the author honors someone
   dedication
3. The part of a book that protects the interior pages
   cover
4. The section of a book that lists words and definitions
   glossary
5. The part of a book that lists what is in the book
   table of contents
6. The name of the person who drew the pictures in a book
   illustrator
7. The part of a book where you could find a list of names
   and subjects in alphabetical order
   index
8. The person who wrote the book
   author

WORD BANK

author	index	glossary	illustrator
table of contents	body	publisher	dedication
copyright page	cover	title page	
place of publication	spine	title	

Parts of a Book

Author	the person who wrote the book
Title	the name of the book
Illustrator	the person who drew the pictures
Place of Publication	the city where the book was published
Publisher	the company that produced the book
Cover	the front and back panels that protect the interior pages
Spine	the hinged side of the book that faces out when the book is on a bookshelf
Title Page	the page at the beginning of the book that includes the title, author, and publisher
Copyright Page	the page that includes all the publishing information, including where and when the book was published and by which company
Dedication	a note in the front of the book in which the author mentions someone's name as a way of honoring them
Table of Contents	a list of what is inside a book and the order in which the items appear
Body	the main text of the book
Glossary	a list of words and definitions at the end of a book
Index	a list of names and subjects in alphabetical order at the end of the book

Name _____ Date _____

 Parts of a Book Quiz

Use the word bank to answer each of these questions.

1. The part of a book that contains the most words

   _____

2. The part of a book where the author honors someone

   _____

3. The part of a book that protects the interior pages

   _____

4. The section of a book that lists words and definitions

   _____

5. The part of a book that lists what is in the book

   _____

6. The name of the person who drew the pictures in a book

   _____

7. The part of a book where you could find a list of names
   and subjects in alphabetical order

   _____

8. The person who wrote the book

   _____

WORD BANK

author	index	glossary	illustrator
table of contents	body	publisher	dedication
copyright page	cover	title page	
place of publication	spine	title	

Parts
of a Book
- Activity -
Nonfiction

A Mini-Book About Books

Materials

- MINI-BOOK template (page 21)
- A QUIZ ABOUT THE PARTS OF A BOOK (page 22)
- sample books
- scissors

Purpose

Students identify the various parts of a book and learn how to use them to locate information.

Directions

1. Pass out copies of the MINI-BOOK template.

2. Show students how to fold the paper into a mini-book, using the directions on page 20.

3. Discuss the different parts of the mini-book with students. Use sample books to compare the mini-book sections with those of actual books.

4. Pass out A QUIZ ABOUT THE PARTS OF A BOOK to assess students' understanding.

Learning About the Parts of a Book

by Ima Writer

Answers to Quiz

1. 9

2. Around the Farm

3. 66–74

4. Springfield, IL

5. Ima Writer

6. relating to or resembling a wolf

7. recipes

8. 29–36

9. 15–28

10. 2007

How to Create the Mini-Books

1. Fold the template in half so that the writing is on the outside of the fold.

2. Fold it in half again in the same direction.

3. Fold this long, narrow strip in half in the opposite direction.

4. Open up the paper to the step 2 position and cut halfway down the vertical fold.

5. Open up the paper and turn it horizontally. There should be a hole in the center where the cut was made.

6. Fold the paper in half lengthwise, writing side facing out.

7. Push in on the ends of the paper so the slit opens up. Push until the center panels meet.

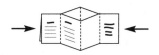

8. Fold the four pages into a little book and crease the binding. Flip through the book and fold it so the title is on the front.

Learning About the Parts of a Book
by Ima Writer

Contents

Dedication
To readers everywhere

ISBN 0-123-45678-1
© 2007 by Ima Writer
All rights reserved.
Printed in the U.S.A.

Learning About the Parts of a Book

by Ima Writer
Illustrations by Art East

Springfield, IL   The Mini-Book Publishing Company

Glossary

adobe–a sun-dried brick of clay and straw

construct–to build

lupine–relating to or resembling a wolf

predator–an animal that hunts other animals

prey–an animal hunted or caught for food

root–to dig in the earth with a snout or nose

wallow–a mud hole made by pigs to keep cool

Index

Learning About the Parts of a Book

by Ima Writer

Name _____ Date _____

 # A Quiz About the Parts of a Book

Use the mini-book *Learning About the Parts of a Book* to answer the following questions.

1. How many chapters are in this book? _____

2. What is the title of the fourth chapter?

   _____

3. On which pages can you learn about playing a flute? _____

4. In which city was this book published?

   _____

5. Who is the author of this book? _____

6. What does the word *lupine* mean?

   _____

7. What information can you find on pages 37–43?

   _____

8. Which pages contain information about big, bad wolves?

   _____

9. On which pages might you find information about ducks,

   sheep, and cows? _____

10. In which year was this book copyrighted? _____

What's in a Name?

Prediction

- Activity -

Fiction

Name *Mary*   Date *May 4*

What's in a Name?

1. Write the title of the book.

The Hello, Goodbye Window

2. What do you think the story is about?

I think the story is about the front
window of someone's house. A man is
in a wheelchair and can't go outside.
He can only look out the window.

3. Read the book. Write a new title for the book.

When I visit Nana and Poppy

4. Explain why you chose this title.

I chose this title because the story is
about a little girl who visits her
granparents.

Materials

- WHAT'S IN A NAME? template (page 24)

Purpose

Students make, confirm, and revise simple predictions about what will be found in a book based on its title.

Directions

1. Pass out a copy of the WHAT'S IN A NAME? template to each student.

2. Read the title of a book aloud and have students write it on the corresponding lines of the template.

3. Ask students to write a sentence that describes what they think the story is about, based solely on the title.

4. Read the story to the class. Discuss students' predictions.

5. Finally, have students write a new title for the book.

Teacher Tip

Help students develop prediction skills by reading an action comic to the class from your local paper for a few weeks. Each day, invite students to predict what will happen in the next day's comic. Ask students to support their predictions with evidence: character traits, story line, dialogue, illustrations, and personal experience.

Name _____ Date _____

What's in a Name?

1. Write the title of the book.

_____

_____

_____

2. What do you think the story is about?

_____

_____

_____

_____

3. Read the book. Write a new title for the book.

_____

_____

_____

4. Explain why you chose this title.

_____

_____

_____

_____

_____

Judging a Book by Its Cover

Materials

- selection of age-appropriate books
- construction paper
- colored markers and pencils

Purpose

Students learn about the elements of a book's cover.

Directions

1. Read the titles of five picture books or novels to the class without showing the covers. Ask students which book they would most like to read and why. Record the votes on the board.

2. Show students the covers of the five books. Ask students whether any of them would like to change their vote. Discuss the elements of a good cover illustration, as well as the elements of a book's cover—the title, author, illustrator, cover illustration, description of story, author's and illustrator's bio, and so on.

3. Read the descriptions of the stories that appear on the back covers or inside flaps. Ask students if any of them would like to change their vote. Discuss the ways in which each paragraph "sells" the book.

4. Read the book that received the most votes.

5. When you are finished reading the book, ask students to fold a sheet of construction paper in half. Invite students to illustrate a new cover for the book. Remind them to include the title and the names of the author and illustrator.

6. Hang the book jackets on a bulletin board under a banner that reads, JUDGING A BOOK BY ITS COVER.

Leveling Tip

Younger students can simply draw a cover illustration that reflects a high point of the book. Older students can include a descriptive paragraph on the back cover and write a review of the book on the interior panels.

Smart Charts

Materials

- SMART CHART template (page 28)
- scissors
- colored pencils and markers
- construction paper
- glue sticks

Purpose

Students will use the K-W-L learning strategy to organize information found in a nonfiction text.

Directions

1. Give each student two copies of the SMART CHART template.

2. Ask students to cut the template in half along the dotted line. They will have four charts but will only use three of them. The fourth can be a spare in case they make a mistake.

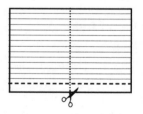

3. Tell students to put the three charts in front of them with the lines faceup. Have them fold the small bottom strip upward along the dashed line and crease it. Then have them fold the top panel down, tuck it under the lower strip, and crease it.

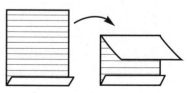

Book Talk

"K-W-L is a teaching model designed to help students learn from nonfiction text in any content area. It consists of a three-step procedure: brainstorming and categorizing, purpose-setting through questioning, and examining answers to those questions."
— Donna Ogle (1986)

4. Instruct students to write the following phrases on the small lower panels of the three smart charts, one phrase for each chart—*What I KNOW, What I WANT to know,* and *What I LEARNED.*

What I KNOW   What I WANT to know   What I LEARNED

5. Before reading a class nonfiction book, ask students to open the smart chart titled *What I KNOW.* Tell students to describe things they already know about the topic they will be studying. On the cover panel of this smart chart, instruct students to draw a picture that illustrates something they know.

6. Then divide the class into small groups. Ask the groups to discuss things they would like to know about the topic. Students can write notes in the smart chart titled *What I WANT to know.* Have them draw a picture that illustrates something they would like to learn about the topic.

7. After reading the nonfiction book, ask students to record things they learned in the third smart chart. On the cover, have students draw an illustration of something they learned while reading the book.

8. Give each student a large sheet of construction paper. Have students cut their sheet into a 7- by 14-inch rectangle. Have them glue their three smart charts onto the construction paper as shown in the sample project on page 26.

9. The finished projects make a nice bulletin board. Add a banner that reads, WHAT WE KNEW AND WHAT WE LEARNED.

Leveling Tip

For an added challenge, have students create a fourth smart chart titled *HOW I will find information.* In this chart, students plan which resources, texts, websites, and trade books they will use to gather information about the topic.

Looking at Pictures

Prediction

- Graphic Organizer -
Fiction

Materials

- storybook or novel with illustrations
- LOOKING AT PICTURES graphic organizer (page 30)

Purpose

Students make, confirm, and revise simple predictions about a story's plot based on the book's illustrations.

Directions

1. Gather together to look at the illustrations from a picture book or novel. As students look at the pictures, ask them to describe what they see, focusing on the characters, objects, settings, and actions.

2. Invite students to fill out the LOOKING AT PICTURES graphic organizer. Students can write a list of nouns and verbs that they see in the pictures. When they are done, ask them to circle the people, objects, places, and actions that they think will play the most important roles in the story line.

3. Encourage students to use evidence that they find in the illustrations to predict the plot of the story.

4. Read the story to the class. Stop reading occasionally and ask students to adjust their predictions if necessary. Discuss the predictions. Which are closest to the actual story? Which are most different?

Book Talk

"Predicting involves more than trying to figure out what happens next. As kids find evidence to form hunches, they also ask questions, recall facts, reread, skim, infer, draw conclusions, and, ultimately, comprehend the text more fully."
— Laura Robb (1996)

Name _____ Date _____

Book Title _____

Looking at Pictures

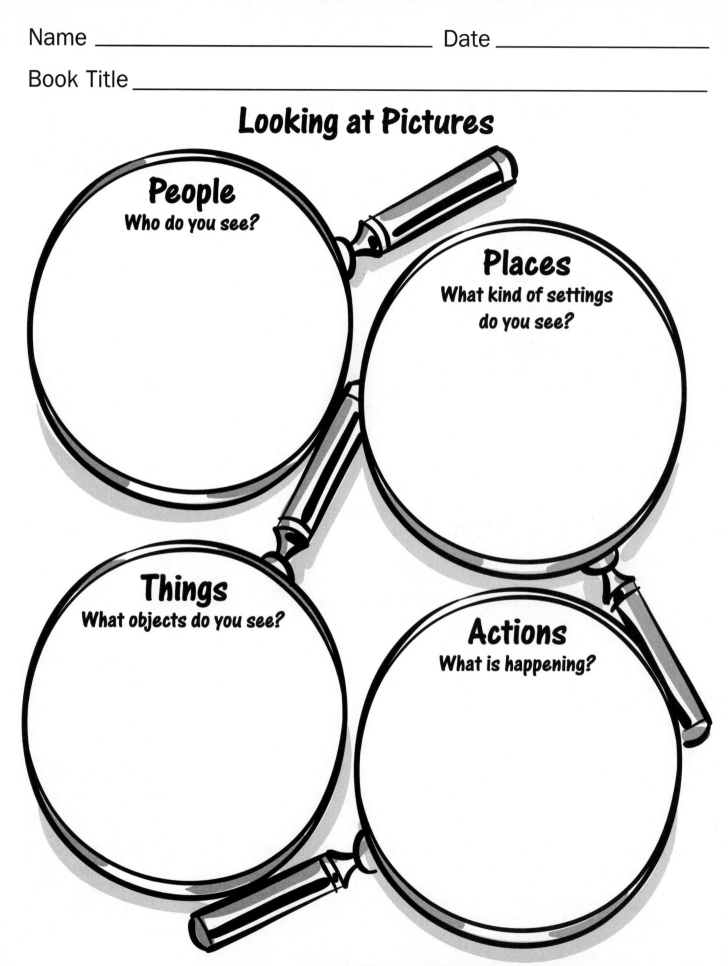

People
Who do you see?

Places
What kind of settings do you see?

Things
What objects do you see?

Actions
What is happening?

Picture Scenes

Materials

- several copies of an illustrated story, chapter book, or textbook

Purpose

Students make, confirm, and revise simple predictions about a story's plot based on the book's illustrations.

Directions

1. Find a chapter book, textbook, or picture book that has illustrations that show moments of action or interest. The pictures should feature several people or animals.

2. Divide the class into groups that have as many members as there are people or animals in the illustration.

3. Give each group a picture. The group members should study the picture and discuss what they think happened immediately before and immediately after the moment shown.

4. After a few minutes of planning, ask each group to improvise a scene that "bookends" the action in the picture. What events led up to the moment shown? What happened after the picture was taken? Tell each group to freeze in the middle of their scene for a few seconds at the point where the picture was taken or drawn.

5. Read the chapter book, storybook, or textbook passage after students have presented scenes to explore how the illustrations enhance the story.

Teacher Tip

Sometimes it's fun to give the same illustration to two different groups to see how their improvisations differ. Compare and contrast their scenes.

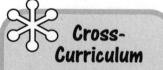

Ending Scenes

Materials

- short stories or picture books

Purpose

Students make "reverse" predictions about a story's plot based on reading the final lines of the story or chapter.

Directions

1. Have students read the last page or paragraph of a short story or picture book. Do this before they've read the full story.

2. Divide the class into groups of five or six students.

3. Ask each group to "think backward" and create a scene that logically leads to the conclusion of the story they just read. Groups will need to create a beginning and middle of the story—they already know how the scene will end.

4. Invite each group to the front of the class to perform their scene. Discuss the reverse predictions that each group created.

5. Read the full story to see how the author chose to tell the story. Compare the author's version with the ones the students created.

Cross-Curriculum

Use ending scenes to encourage creative thinking and deductive reasoning in your social studies classroom. Discuss the ending moment of an event (such as colonists throwing boxes of tea into Boston Harbor). Have the groups create a scene that describes why they think the colonists would do such a thing. Their scene should end with the Boston Tea Party. Then read the section of your textbook that details the actual happenings of this historic event.

Turn-to-Learn Story Elements

Main Character

Little Miss Muffet

TURN-TO-LEARN

STORY ELEMENTS

Materials

- TURN-TO-LEARN templates (pages 34–36)
- scissors
- brass paper fasteners
- colored markers and pencils

Purpose

Students learn about story elements—main character, setting, action, antagonist, problem, and solution.

Directions

1. As a prereading activity, make copies of TURN-TO-LEARN templates 1 and 2 and pass them out to students.

2. Have students cut out the disks. An adult should cut out the square window on disk 1.

3. Show students how to place disk 1 on top of disk 2 and push a brass paper fastener through the center dots to attach them together.

4. Have everyone rotate the top disk as you read the story of Little Miss Muffet. Focus on the story elements.

5. As a postreading activity, make copies of templates 1 and 3, and have students cut them out and attach them together with a brass paper fastener.

6. On the cover of the disk, have them write their name and the title of the book they read. Encourage them to draw a picture related to the story.

7. Have students write a few words about each of the book's story elements in the upper window. In the lower window, they can draw an icon that represents each element.

Teacher Tip

To make a sturdy version of the wheel for your learning center, glue disks to a sheet of oaktag before cutting them out. (An adult will need to cut out the windows with a craft knife.) Color and laminate the wheels before attaching them with a brass paper fastener.

Name _____ Date _____

Turn-to-Learn Story Elements Template 1

cut out this window

TURN-TO-LEARN

STORY
ELEMENTS

cut out
this
window

Name _____ Date _____

Turn-to-Learn Story Elements Template 2

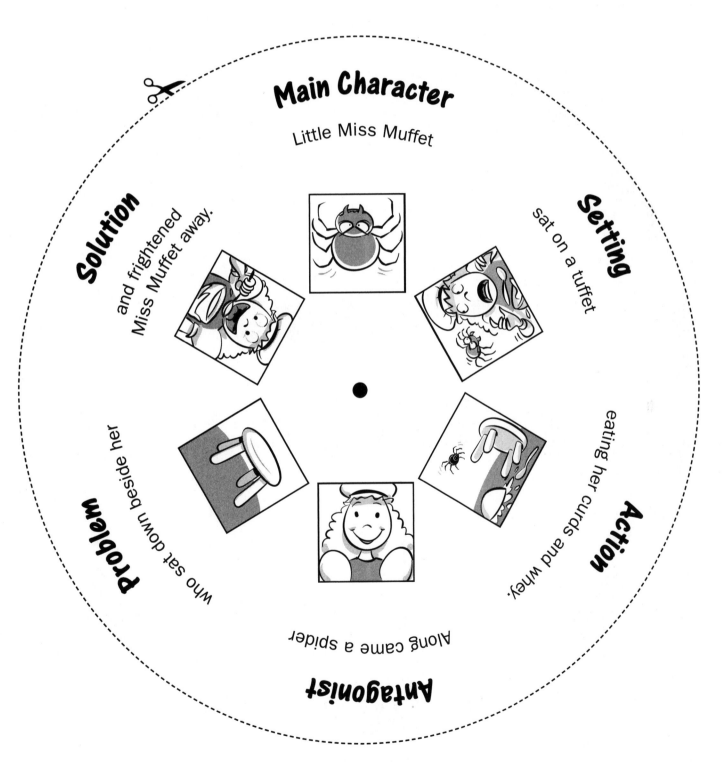

Main Character

Little Miss Muffet

Setting

sat on a tuffet

Solution

and frightened Miss Muffet away.

Action

eating her curds and whey.

Problem

who sat down beside her

Antagonist

Along came a spider

Name _____ Date _____

Turn-to-Learn Story Elements Template 3

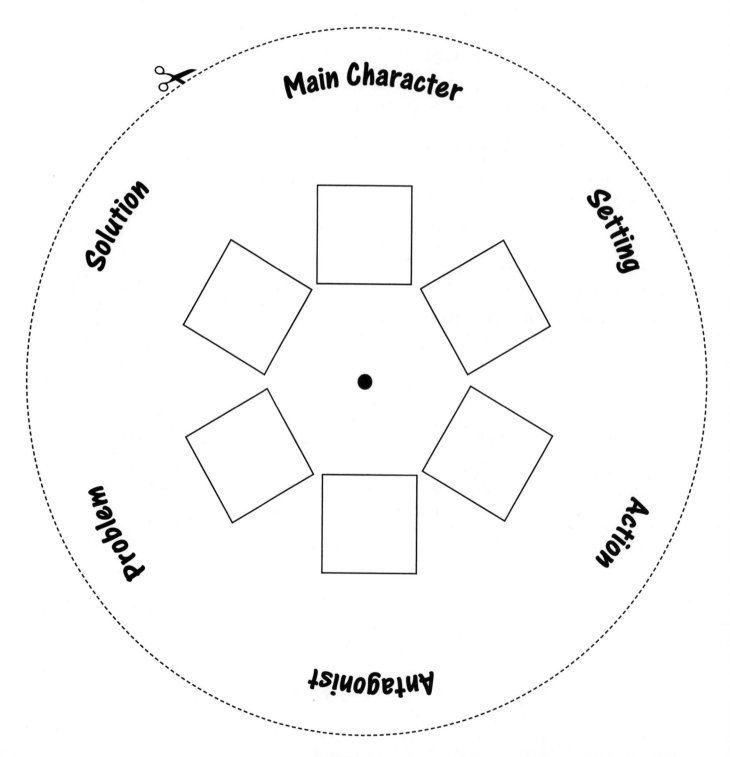

Telling Tales

Group
Storytelling
- Creative Dramatics -
Fiction

Purpose

Students demonstrate a knowledge of basic story elements as they create an oral story in a whole-group setting.

Directions

1. Invite students to sit in a circle—on the floor, at their desks, or outside—so everyone can see one another.

2. Discuss the elements of a story—such as, a story has a beginning, middle, and end; characters and setting are revealed toward the beginning; problems are introduced; and a solution is given toward the end.

3. Ask a student to say a complete sentence that could be the first line of a story.

4. The student sitting next to the first student says another complete sentence to continue the story.

5. One by one, each student adds a complete sentence to the story until the last student says the final line of the story.

6. Discuss the fact that the first student had no idea where the story was going to go plotwise, and that the story took a different turn each time a student created a sentence. Help students understand that a story can go anywhere our imagination takes us.

Teacher Tip

This activity is a perfect warm-up exercise for a creative writing class. Start each session by having the class create an extemporaneous story to help students understand that taking a story in an unexpected direction can help them overcome writer's block.

Types of Books
- Graphic Organizer -
Fiction/Nonfiction

Introducing Genre

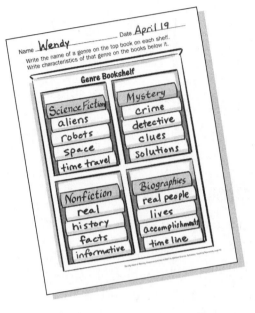

Name Wendy   Date April 19
Write the name of a genre on the top book on each shelf.
Write characteristics of that genre on the books below it.

Genre Bookshelf

Science Fiction
aliens
robots
space
time travel

Mystery
crime
detective
clues
solutions

Nonfiction
real
history
facts
informative

Biographies
real people
lives
accomplishments
time line

Book Talk

"The analysis of different types of literature promotes cognitive development because it gives students an opportunity to apply similar skills and strategies, such as identifying themes discussed in one genre—fiction, for example—to other genres like poetry, reports, descriptive pieces, and plays."
— Carl B. Smith (1991)

Teacher Tip

Describe ways in which genres can overlap. For example, a piece of historical fiction can also be a mystery. Or a western can also contain elements of an adventure novel.

Materials

- GENRE BOOKSHELF graphic organizer (page 40)

Purpose

Students learn about the basic characteristics of familiar genres.

Directions

1. Give each student a copy of the GENRE BOOKSHELF graphic organizer.

2. Choose four different genres that you would like to discuss with the class. See the suggested list of genres and characteristics on page 39.

3. Have students write the names of different genres on the top book of each shelf.

4. Have students write four characteristics of each genre on the books underneath.

Suggested Genres and Characteristics

Adventure/Suspense—travel, realistic settings, journeys, quests, physical action, tense, villains, heroic main character, big obstacles, page-turner, cliffhangers at end of each chapter, fast paced, exciting, danger, twists and turns

Biographies—the story of a person's life, factual, autobiography, nonfiction, feats and accomplishments, major events

Drama—realistic characters, slow pace, happy or sad ending, strong emotions, serious

Fantasy—magical creatures, different worlds, dragons, magic, elves, fairies, unicorns, unreal, animals with human characteristics

Folktales, Fables, and Fairy Tales—passed down through generations, talking animals, moral lessons, princesses, magical

Historical Fiction—based a real event or time, set in the past, strong sense of place and time, realistic

Horror—scary, monsters and scary creatures, fear, page-turner, aliens, nightmares

Humor—funny, jokes, comedy, joke books, absurd situations, zany characters

Mystery—puzzles, clues, sleuths, detectives, red herrings, crime, "whodunit," suspicious characters, suspense, solution, twists, surprises, spies

Myths and Legends—explanations of how natural things (such as the world or the sun) were created, magical, giants, gods and goddesses, Greece, stories from long ago

Nonfiction—informational, factual, how things work, history, science, biographies,

Picture Books—illustrations, easy-to-read, younger children, short

Poetry—verse, rhyme, figurative language, humorous or serious, lyrical or narrative, rhythm, meter, imagery

Science Fiction—technology, future, space, distant worlds, scientists, laboratories, danger, aliens, robots, time travel, computers, spaceships

Tall Tales—far-fetched, exaggeration, larger-than-life characters, legendary characters, heroes, superhuman abilities, funny, lots of action

Westerns—cowboys, outlaws, Native Americans, Old West, frontier towns, prairies, buffalo, horses, wagon trains

Name _____ Date _____

Write the name of a genre on the top book in each shelf.
Write characteristics of that genre on the books below it.

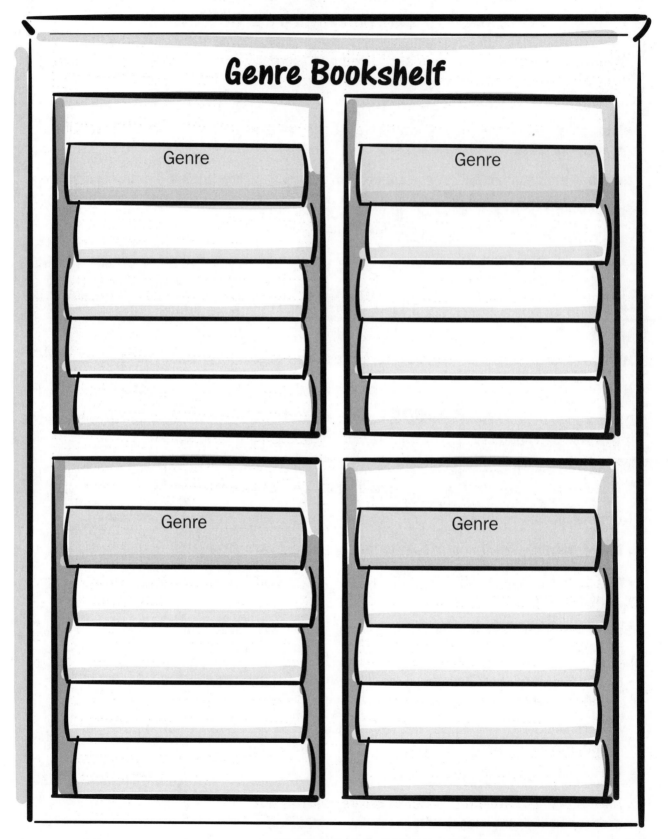

Genre Bookshelf

Genre

Genre

Genre

Genre

First Lines

Prediction

- Activity -

Fiction

First Lines template worksheet showing handwritten student responses

Materials

- FIRST LINES template (page 42)

Purpose

Students make predictions about a story's plot based on the book's first lines.

Directions

1. Discuss the following two classic first lines with the class. Ask: "What does it tell us about the story? Who is the story about? How does it make you feel?"

   All children, except one, grow up. —*Peter Pan*

   "Where's Pa going with that ax?" —*Charlotte's Web*

2. Pass out a copy of the FIRST LINES template to each student. (You could write the title of the book and its first line(s) on the template prior to copying it, or you could have students do this.)

3. Read the first line(s) of the book aloud. Have students answer the questions on the template.

4. After students have written their answers, discuss the responses with the class.

Book Talk

"Skilled readers consciously try to anticipate what the text is about before they begin reading. They look at the cover, art, title, genre, author, headings, graphs, charts, length, print size, front flaps, and back covers."
—Kylene Beers (2003)

Teacher Tip

Before selecting a story to read aloud to the class, read the first lines from several books to students. Discuss the lines with the them. Ask: "What might the story be about? What genre do you think this is? Did the author pique your interest?" Allow students to choose which story you will read aloud.

Name ______________________________ Date ____________________

First Lines

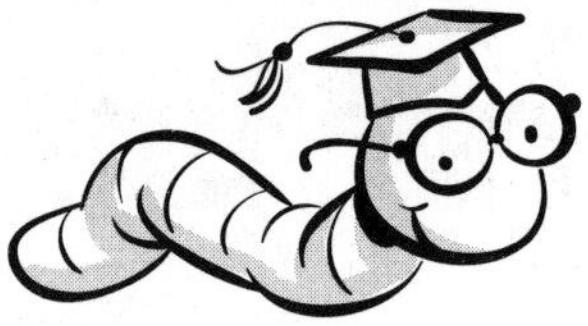

1. Write the title of the book.

2. Write the first line from the book.

3. How does the first line from this book make you feel?

4. What do you think you know about this book from the first line?

Five Words

Using
Vocabulary
- Creative Dramatics -
Fiction/Nonfiction

What a difficult journey! We've climbed a mountain and crossed a canyon.

visible
canyon
ancestor
appetite
journey

Materials

- index cards

Purpose

Students learn the meanings of new vocabulary words and use them in the context of a short, improvised scene.

Directions

1. Divide all the new vocabulary words that students will have to learn for an upcoming chapter book or story into sets of five.

2. Write each set of five words on a different index card.

3. Divide the class into groups of four or five and give each group an index card.

4. Instruct the groups to look up the definitions for each of the words on their card and write them down.

5. Then ask the groups to create a short scene, complete with a beginning, a middle, and an end, in which the five words are used in a way so their meanings are understood.

6. After each group has performed, ask the other students to tell the meanings of the vocabulary words used in the skit. Discuss and define further if necessary.

7. As you come across each word while reading the story, reflect back to this activity. Discuss the way the word was used in the skit and how it is used in the story.

Teacher Tip

Creative dramatics promotes social skills because it stimulates discussions as students work together to solve a problem. The more often you have students perform in front of their peers, the more confident they will become with public speaking as well.

Making Books

Materials

- LINED PAGE template (page 46)
- scissors
- construction paper
- hole punch
- yarn or ribbon
- beads (optional)
- colored markers or pencils

Cross-Curriculum

Scrapbooking stores sell sheets of paper that feature themed illustrations. These can be used for covers of student-made books that relate to many subjects—from sports to space and from art to America.

Leveling Tip

Younger students may have trouble folding the pages evenly, so you might want to conduct this activity with the help of a parent or an aide.

Purpose

Students construct bound books in which they can write and illustrate stories.

Directions

1. Make two-sided copies of the LINED PAGE template. The lines on the back side should appear directly behind the lines on the front side.

2. Cut construction paper (or another type of decorative paper) so that it is slightly larger than the template page. This will serve as the cover of the finished book.

3. Give each student a cover sheet and a template sheet. (Each template will make four pages in the finished book. For longer books, give students more template sheets.)

4. Show students how to place the templates on top of the cover sheet and fold them in half to create the book.

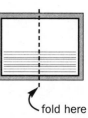

fold here

5. After students have folded their paper, walk around with the hole punch and punch three holes down the fold of each student's book. Be sure to punch *half* holes, so when the book is opened a full hole will appear.

6. Give each student a 2-foot length of yarn or ribbon. Ask them to thread the yarn through the center hole from the exterior to the interior of the book.

7. Have them continue threading the yarn through the top hole, from the interior to the exterior.

8. Tell students to continue threading the yarn through the bottom hole, from the exterior to the interior.

9. Have them thread the yarn back through the center hole.

10. Thread the ends of the yarn through a decorative bead and tie a knot. (If you don't have beads, simply tie the two ends around the length of yarn that runs from the top hole to the bottom hole. This will prevent the knot from being pulled back through the center hole.)

11. Trim the excess yarn with scissors.

12. Have students write a story on the lines at the bottom of each page. Invite them to draw a picture in the space at the top of each page.

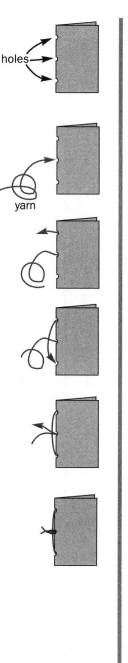

Teacher Tip

When children create their own books, it gives them a sense of ownership and makes them more likely to look at their work over and over again. Add the student-made books to your class library to help students understand that they are authors who should be proud of their work.

Parts of a Whole

Main Idea
and Details
- Creative Dramatics -
Nonfiction

Materials

- index cards

Purpose

Students play a theater game to show their knowledge of the main idea and supporting details of a particular topic.

Directions

1. Use this activity as a warm-up before reading about a nonfiction curricular topic, such as the four seasons, community helpers, transportation, or types of weather.

2. On index cards, write subcategories of the topic; for example, if the topic is the four seasons, the index cards could read "winter," "spring," "summer," and "fall;" if the topic is transportation, the cards could read "by air," "by land," and "by sea."

3. Divide the class into as many groups as you have subcategories. Give each group a card.

4. Instruct each group member to pantomime a different aspect of the subcategory on their index card (using no words or sounds). For example, if the subcategory is summer, the group members could pantomime swimming, building sand castles, eating ice cream, cutting the grass, jumping rope, and reading a book. Allow a few minutes for the groups to plan what each member will do.

5. Invite each group to perform their pantomimes, one at a time. Challenge the other groups to guess the subcategory on the card and what each group member is doing.

6. After each group has performed, ask the class to brainstorm other activities that fit each category.

7. Finally, read a nonfiction book to learn more about the subject.

Teacher Tip

Group pantomime is a great way to encourage shyer students to perform in front of the class. The security of being in a group and the fact that no talking is involved helps the reluctant student feel safe. Once students begin to feel comfortable, introduce dialogue to the creative dramatics activities. Soon, even your shyest students will be acting out scenes from class novels.

You've Got Mail!

Materials

- MAILBOX template (page 50)
- scissors
- colored pencils or markers
- manila folders
- glue sticks
- brass paper fasteners

Purpose

Students create an interactive bulletin board to strengthen their understanding that reading and writing are used to communicate ideas.

Directions

1. Give each student a manila folder and a copy of the MAILBOX template. Have students cut out the mailbox and flag.

2. Instruct students to color the mailbox and flag and write their name in creative letters in the rectangle on the side of the mailbox.

3. Show students how to glue the mailbox onto the manila folder so that the bottom of the mailbox aligns with the folded edge.

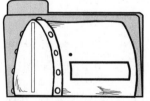

✎ Teacher Tip

Have students use the mailboxes to send notes, cards, letters, and valentines to classmates.

4. Have them cut out the mailbox, making sure that they are cutting both sides of the manila folder. When they are done, they will have a folder in the shape of a mailbox.

5. Instruct students to glue the flag onto a large scrap of manila folder and cut it out.

6. Have students place the flag on top of the mailbox so the two black dots align and then push a brass paper fastener through the black dots. (An adult should complete this step for students.) Only fasten the flag to the top panel of the manila folder. The flag can now be lifted and lowered to indicate whether or not there is mail in the box.

Push the brass paper fastener through the top panel of the folder only.

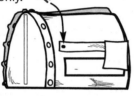

7. Cut out the mail slot on the left side of the mailbox. Only cut the slot from the top panel of the manila folder. (An adult should complete this step.)

8. Show students how to glue the top and side edges of the manila mailbox closed. Letters can now be inserted into the slot without falling out.

9. Hang a banner on the bulletin board that reads, YOU'VE GOT MAIL! Under the banner add the mailboxes. You might want to have students make "wooden" posts out of construction paper for the mailboxes to sit on.

Teacher Tip

Invite students to write a letter discussing their goals for the coming school year. Have them address it to their parents and put it in their mailbox. On back-to-school night, have parents get the letter from their child's mailbox, read it, and write a response for their child to pick up the next day.

You've Got Mail!

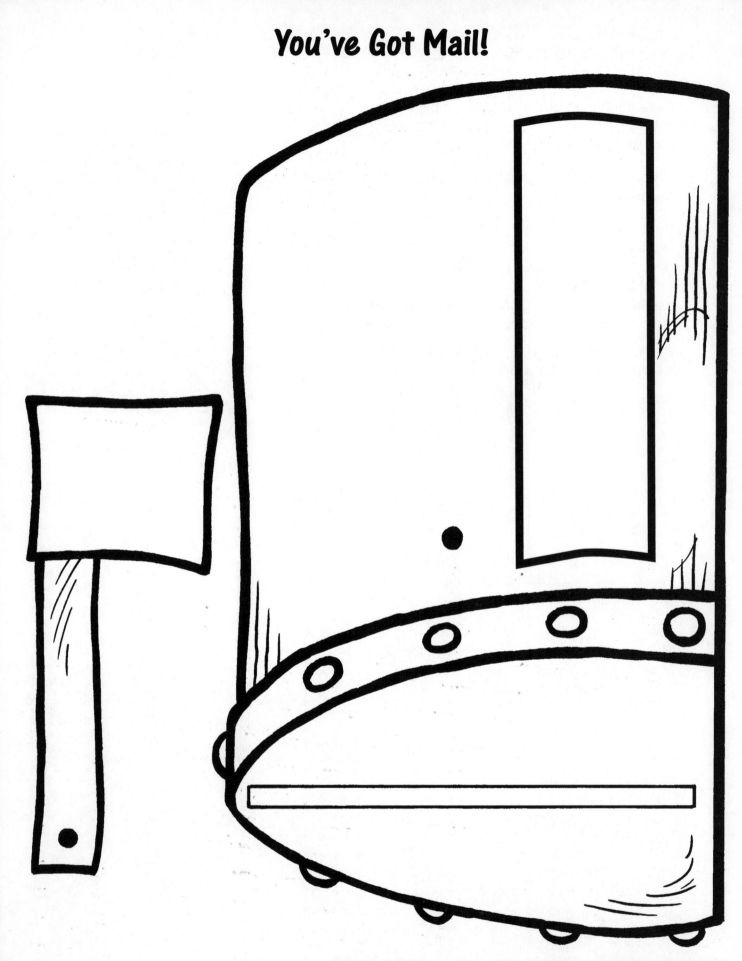

Weekly Reading Contract

Independent Reading
- Graphic Organizer -
Fiction/Nonfiction

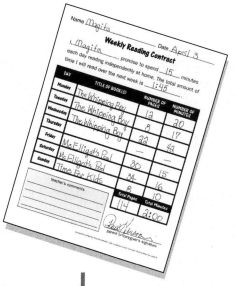

Materials

- WEEKLY READING CONTRACT template (page 52)

Purpose

Students implement a plan to read for a proposed period of time.

Directions

1. Pass out copies of the WEEKLY READING CONTRACT to students on a Monday morning.

2. Ask students to write the number of minutes they plan to spend reading at home each day and the total length of time they will read over the next week. Visit the school library regularly so students have access to a variety of books.

3. Each evening, students fill out the number of minutes and the number of pages they read independently that day.

4. The following Sunday evening, students add up the total number of minutes and pages they read the previous week. Instruct students to have a parent or caregiver sign the contract.

5. Collect the contracts on Monday morning and keep them in students' reading folders. During individual conferences, work with students to assess their progress and to determine the amount of time they should read the following week.

Teacher Tip

After students complete each week's reading contract, encourage them to write a short response on the back of the contract. They can describe the selection they most enjoyed reading, how it made them feel, or whether it was too easy or difficult.

Name _____ Date _____

Weekly Reading Contract

I, _____, promise to spend _____ minutes each day reading independently at home. The total amount of time I will read over the next week is _____ .

DAY	TITLE OF BOOK(S)	NUMBER OF PAGES	NUMBER OF MINUTES
Monday			
Tuesday			
Wednesday			
Thursday			
Friday			
Saturday			
Sunday			
		Total Pages	**Total Minutes**

Teacher's Comments

_____
_____
_____
_____

_____
Parent's or Caregiver's Signature

A Family of Readers

Home/School
Connections
- Activity -
Fiction/Nonfiction

Materials

- LETTER TO FAMILIES (page 54)
- canvas bags
- books
- stuffed animals
- CHECK OUT THIS BOOK! form (page 55)
- BOOK TRAIN template (page 56)

Purpose

This activity encourages students to read at home.

Directions

1. Make copies of the letter to families on page 57. This letter explains how parents and caregivers can help in their child's literacy development and explains the at-home reading program. Send a copy home with each child.

2. Collect canvas bags and fill each one with five or six books. Consider sorting books by theme or genre and labeling each bag with the type of books it contains (humor, animal stories, seasonal, mystery, space, and so on).

3. Place a small stuffed animal in each bag. (Assorted animals or dolls could be called "book buddies," beanbag insects could be called "snuggle bugs," and so on.)

4. Send the canvas bags home with several students each night. Encourage students to read to their book buddy or to a family member whenever they take a bag home. Invite families to read the books to their child.

5. In the bag, include a copy of the BOOK TRAIN template. Ask parents and students to color the engine of the train and fill out a car for each book the child reads. (Additional copies of the cars can be sent home as needed.) Encourage students to display the train at home to track the number of books they read over the course of the year.

6. Also provide a copy of the CHECK OUT THIS BOOK! template. Parents and students can fill out a form whenever they want to keep a book for a longer period.

Leveling Tip

Include books written at a variety of reading levels (easy readers, picture books, and longer chapter books). Allow students to check out a book for longer periods if they have not finished reading it.

Dear Families,

I am writing to introduce you to my at-home reading program and to offer suggestions of ways you can nurture a love of reading in your child. Every couple of weeks your child will take home a bag of books with a *book buddy*—a stuffed toy that serves as an audience to your child's reading. I encourage you, too, to become an audience member and listen to your child read. But I also encourage you to become a participant by reading the more difficult books to your child.

Feel free to keep the book until you complete it. Just drop a note in the bag—using the attached form—letting me know which books you're keeping and I'll place it in my "Checked Out" file. Whenever your child finishes a book, please record it on a car from the Book Train form and cut it out. Display the train in your home so your child can watch the train grow longer and longer throughout the year.

With all of life's distractions—hundreds of television channels, video games, megamalls, and so on—it is especially hard for today's child to choose reading. Here are some ways that you can help:

- **Be a model reader**—Let your child see you read. Read newspapers, magazines, and books of all types. Point out interesting things you read. Discuss words that sound playful or unusual. Comment on the way a writer uses language. Ask your child questions as you read. And read to your child often. Reading aloud not only allows your child to hear your voice, explore the beauty of language, and learn how to be expressive, but it also provides an incredible bonding experience.

- **Make regular trips to the library**—Get a library card for your child. Help in the selection of books. Examine the covers together. Read a few lines from each book. Read the synopsis. Look at the pictures. Allow your child to choose the books he or she reads.

- **Let your child read to you**—Provide positive feedback about your child's reading skills. Ask general comprehension questions, but without turning it into a lesson. Reading at home should not feel like school. Please consult me if you notice any problems.

- **Provide a range of reading materials**—Check out fiction and nonfiction books from the library that echo subjects and themes being taught in school. Even if your child only flips through the books, he or she will learn to turn to books for information.

Reading—like playing an instrument or excelling at a sport—is a skill that improves with practice. Research shows that children who read daily are more likely to do better in school and become readers later in life. Let's work together to ensure that your child becomes a lifelong reader.

Sincerely,

Name _____ Date _____

Check Out This Book!

Use these forms if you want to keep one of the class books at home until you have finished it.

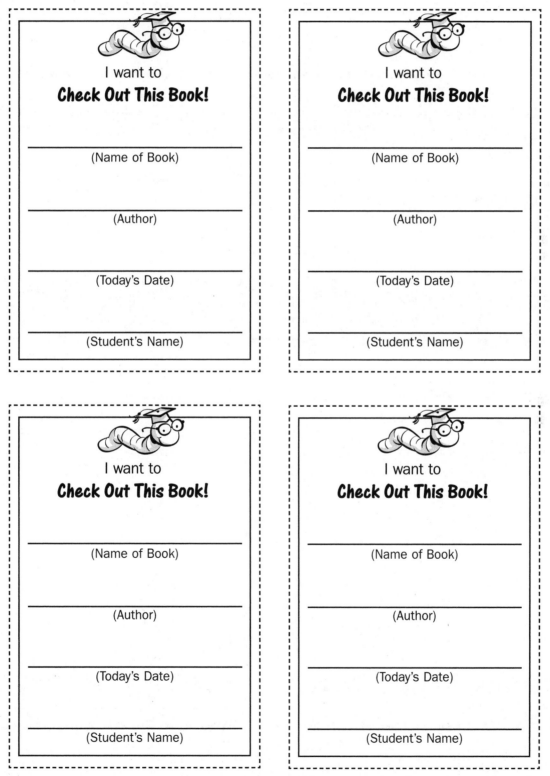

I want to
Check Out This Book!

_____
(Name of Book)

_____
(Author)

_____
(Today's Date)

_____
(Student's Name)

I want to
Check Out This Book!

_____
(Name of Book)

_____
(Author)

_____
(Today's Date)

_____
(Student's Name)

I want to
Check Out This Book!

_____
(Name of Book)

_____
(Author)

_____
(Today's Date)

_____
(Student's Name)

I want to
Check Out This Book!

_____
(Name of Book)

_____
(Author)

_____
(Today's Date)

_____
(Student's Name)

The Big Book of Reading Response Activities © 2007 by Michael Gravois, Scholastic Teaching Resources, page 55

Name _____ Date _____

Book Train

All Aboard! Color the engine and hang it on your wall. Every time you finish a book, fill out one of the cars and add it to the train. Watch the train grow and grow as you become an expert reader!

Your Name

Name of Book

Author

Date Finished

Name of Book

Author

Date Finished

Reading Response Logs

Writing About
Reading
- Activity -
Fiction/Nonfiction

Materials

- READING RESPONSE LOG templates (pages 60–61)
- colored pencils or markers
- three-hole-punch copier paper
- brass paper fasteners
- construction paper
- hole punch

Purpose

Students write in response to literature (summarize main ideas, advance judgements, make connections, and so on).

Directions

1. Look over the sample reading response prompts listed on pages 58–59. Choose one of these or create one of your own.

2. Write the prompt on one of the READING RESPONSE LOG templates on pages 60–61. Use the art template if artwork is required. Use the writing template if the response is to be written.

3. Make copies of the template on three-hole-punch copier paper and give a copy to each student.

4. Ask students to respond to the prompt.

5. As students complete pages, show them how to fasten the pages together with brass paper fasteners. More pages can be added as students complete them.

6. Invite students to use construction paper and colored markers to create a cover for their reading response log. Use a hole punch to punch three holes in the construction paper so they can be added to the logs.

Leveling Tip

Allow students who have difficulty writing to speak into a tape recorder in the classroom. Have them use an egg timer to keep their responses concise. Children enjoy talking into a recorder, and this activity allows you to give your undivided attention to individual students. It also provides you with an oral record of the students' work. Make sure students begin each response by stating their name, the date, and the question they're answering.

Reading Response Prompts

Type of Prompt	Sample Prompt
Recall	- Summarize the chapter you just read. - Draw a picture of the climax of the story. - List five adjectives that describe the main character in the book. - Describe the setting of the story. Illustrate it. - What is the major problem the main character faces? How is it resolved?
Prediction	- How do you think the story will end? - Which character do you think will change the most by the end? Why? - Who do you think the culprit is? - Based on the title of the book, what do you think the book is about? - Look at the illustrations. What do they tell you about the book? - Draw a picture of what you think will happen next. Describe it in a sentence.
Making Connections	- How is this book similar to another you have read by this author? - Which character is most like you? In what ways are you similar? - Create a Venn diagram that compares the setting of this story to the surroundings where you live. - How have you changed after reading this book? - What were your feelings after reading the first chapter of this book? - Draw and describe an event from your life that was like an event that happened in the story. - What advice would you give a character in this book? Why? - Which character would you most like to meet? Why? - Write an e-mail that you would like to send to the author. - Compare a character in this book to a character from another book you've read. - Describe a character's personality trait that you'd like to possess. Why do you like this trait?

Reading Response Prompts

Type of Prompt	Sample Prompt
Opinion	- Why do you think the author chose the opening line she did? Do you like it? Did it make you want to read further? - Who is your favorite character? Why? Draw a picture of this character. - What do you think of the antagonist's actions? Why? - What do you think is the most important scene in the book? Why? - How would a different setting affect the story? - Was the cover design effective? Did it make you want to read the book? Create a cover design that you think readers would like. - Did you like the ending of the book? How would you have liked it to end? Write a new ending for the book. - Write a question you would like to ask the author. How do you think he would respond?
Language	- Write five words that you find interesting or unfamiliar. Write their definitions and use each in a sentence. - Copy a sentence from the book that you think is well written. Why do you like this sentence? Illustrate the sentence. - Find examples of descriptive language in the text. Write them down. - What is your favorite line spoken by a character? Why do you like it?
Evaluation	- Did you enjoy the book? Why or why not? - Was the book hard or easy to read? Why? - What didn't you understand about the story? I'll respond to your questions when I check your log. - What do you know now that you didn't know before? - Describe your feelings after finishing the book. - Would you like to read more books by this author? Why or why not? - Do you think the author chose a good title for the book? Why or why not? - What did you learn about the time in which the story took place?

Name _____ Date _____

Reading Response Log Art Template

Prompt: _____

_____

_____

_____

_____

_____

_____

_____

_____

Name _____ Date _____

Reading Response Log Writing Template

Prompt: _____

_____

_____

_____

_____

_____

_____

_____

_____

_____

_____

_____

_____

_____

_____

_____

Is That a Fact?

Fiction and Nonfiction
- Graphic Organizer -
Fiction/Nonfiction

Name Stacy   Date April 15

Is That a Fact?

Bat Facts

Bats are mammals.
They are nocturnal.
They hide in hollow trees, caves, and rock crevices.
Some eat fruit.

They are the only mammals to truly fly.
Some eat insects.
Bats are color blind.
They can live twenty to thirty years.

Materials

- Is THAT A FACT? graphic organizer (page 64)
- text sets (paired fiction and nonfiction books on a similar topic)

Purpose

Students demonstrate knowledge of the difference between fact and fiction.

Directions

1. Ask your school librarian to help you find fiction and nonfiction books related to a topic you're studying. (The example of "bats" is used below. See the suggested list of bat books on page 63.)

2. Draw a T-chart on the board. Write the words "fiction" and "nonfiction" on opposite sides of the chart.

fiction	nonfiction

3. Lead a class discussion about the differences between fiction and nonfiction (defining them if necessary). List examples on the T-chart.

4. Tell students that you are going to read them a fiction book about bats. Explain that factual information can often be found in books that are classified as fiction. Ask students to listen for any information in the story about bats that might be true.

5. Read *Stellaluna* by Janell Cannon.

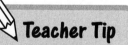

Teacher Tip

Some students feel more comfortable reading narrative fiction than nonfiction. Using text sets helps bridge these two genres, giving these students the confidence to explore the less familiar format of nonfiction.

6. Give each student two copies of the Is THAT A FACT? graphic organizer. Have students label one graphic organizer "Bat Facts" and the other "Bat Fiction."

7. Challenge students to identify facts about bats that they heard in the story and write them on the bat labeled "Bat Facts." (For example, bats sleep upside down, can see at night, and eat fruit.)

8. Ask students to identify fictitious elements in the story and write them on the bat labeled "Bat Fiction." (For example, bats and birds don't live together, animals don't talk, and birds wouldn't try to hang by their feet.)

9. Tell students that you are going to read a nonfiction book about bats. Explain that they can learn a lot more factual information when they read a nonfiction book. Read *Bats* by Gail Gibbons.

10. Ask students to identify facts they remember from the book. Instruct them to write these facts on the graphic organizer labeled "Bat Facts."

11. Encourage students to color the bats and cut them out. Staple the bodies to a bulletin board, allowing the wings to pop up.

BAT BOOKS

Fiction

Bat Jamboree by Kathi Appelt (HarperTrophy, 1998)
The Magic Schoolbus: Going Batty by Joanna Cole (Scholastic, 1996)
Stellaluna by Janell Cannon (Harcourt Children's Books, 1993)

Nonfiction

Bat Loves the Night by Nicola Davies (Candlewick, 2001)
Bats by Gail Gibbons (Holiday House, 2000)
Bats by Lily Wood (Scholastic, 2001)
Bats: Creatures of the Night by Joyce Milton (Grosset and Dunlap, 1993)
Little Bat by Tania Cox (Working Title Press, 1999)
Zipping, Zapping, Zooming Bats by Ann Earle (HarperTrophy, 1995)

Teacher Tip

Sometimes when we read fiction books, what we *think* may be factual information is actually not accurate. You can teach this concept by having the students read a fiction book and label a copy of the graphic organizer "Things we *think* are facts," under which they can list the facts they learned. They can then read a nonfiction book and label another copy of the graphic organizer "Things we *know* are facts," under which they can list the facts they learned. Sometimes students may have to adjust and amend the information they wrote on the first organizer after reading the nonfiction book.

Name _____

Date _____

Is That a Fact?

Freeze-Frames

Identifying the
Main Idea
- Creative Dramatics -
Fiction/Nonfiction

Materials

- index cards

Purpose

Students work in small groups to create frozen poses that convey the main ideas of a story.

Directions

1. Write the titles of well-known nursery rhymes on index cards, for example "Little Bo Peep," "Hey Diddle Diddle," and "Rub-a-Dub-Dub."

2. Divide the class into groups of four or five, and give each group an index card.

3. Ask each group to create a single freeze-frame—a living snapshot of a moment of action—that conveys the main idea of the nursery rhyme they picked. Students can act like people, animals, or inanimate objects.

4. After groups have had time to plan their freeze-frame, choose a group to go first. Count to three and tell the group to freeze, as if a snapshot were taken at a moment of action.

5. Invite other groups to guess the nursery rhyme that the freeze-frame illustrates.

Cross-Curriculum

Challenge students to create freeze-frames that highlight the main idea of famous events in American history or science, such as George Washington crossing the Delaware or the Wright brothers at Kittyhawk. If other students are having difficulty guessing the event, "interview" the actors in the freeze-frame. Say, "Tell me sir, what are you thinking right now?" or "Madam, what are you doing at this moment?" By tracking the thoughts of the characters in the freeze-frame, you're asking the actors to step into the mind of the person they're representing.

Teacher Tip

Introduce students to the idea of improvisation. When a group is performing a freeze-frame, tell the actors that you have a magical remote and you're going to push the play button. When you say, "Play," the group starts acting out the scene, using movement and dialogue. You can also pause, rewind, fast-forward, or mute the action. When students perform a scene without the benefit of a script, they learn how to improvise.

6. Then pass out index cards that contain the titles of famous fairy tales, for example "Cinderella," "Little Red Riding Hood," and "Hansel and Gretel."

7. Instruct each group to create three separate freeze-frames, conveying the main idea of the beginning, the middle, and the end of the story.

8. After the group creates the first freeze-frame, ask other students to raise their hand if they think they know which fairy tale the group is performing. Tell students not to call out the title. Repeat this after each freeze-frame.

9. After the third freeze-frame, ask students to identify the fairy tale. Invite the class to offer suggestions for other things that could have been acted out in each scene that might help convey the main idea.

10. Now that the class knows how the activity works, use it as a way to check for understanding while reading a class novel or story. Groups can create a freeze-frame that conveys the main idea of a chapter you just finished, or they can create a "prediction freeze-frame" that illustrates what the group thinks will happen in the next chapter. You can have each group create five freeze-frames showing major events from the story or two freeze-frames that convey the plot's major problem and solution.

Character Maps

Character
Traits
- Graphic Organizer -
Fiction

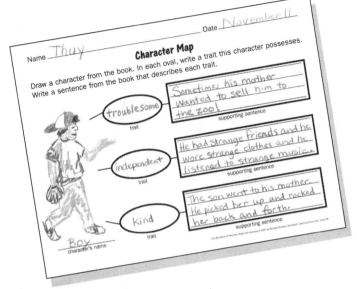

Materials

- CHARACTER MAP graphic organizer (page 68)
- crayons or colored pencils

Purpose

Students identify key traits of a character from a story they are reading.

Directions

1. Pass out a copy of the CHARACTER MAP graphic organizer to each student.

2. Ask students to use crayons or colored pencils to draw a character from a book they are reading. Have them write the character's name under the illustration.

3. In each of the ovals, have students write one character trait the character possesses.

4. On the lines to the right of each oval, instruct students to write a sentence from the book that supports their claim.

Teacher Tip

Studying the traits of protagonists and antagonists helps students understand qualities that they can develop or reject in themselves. After students have filled out their graphic organizers, discuss the traits that different characters possess. Ask students which traits are positive and which are negative. Encourage students to describe ways in which they can adopt the positive ones.

Name _____

Date _____

Character Map

Draw a character from the book. In each oval, write a trait this character possesses.
Write a sentence from the book that describes each trait.

trait

supporting sentence

trait

supporting sentence

trait

supporting sentence

character's name

The Big Book of Reading Response Activities © 2007 by Michael Gravois, Scholastic Teaching Resources, page 68

Character Cards

Materials

- 8¹/₂- by 11-inch white cardstock
- colored pencils or markers
- scissors

Purpose

Students create character cards to demonstrate their understanding of character development in literary works.

Directions

1. Give one sheet of white cardstock to every two students, and have one of the students cut it in half vertically. Each student will now have one vertical half sheet. (Students can vary the height and width of the rectangle to create different shapes for their character cards.)

2. Ask students to fold their paper in half vertically.

3. Have students draw the shoulder and head of their character at the top and a foot at the bottom (as shown at right). Then have students cut out the figure, making sure to cut both sides of the card.

4. Ask students to open the card and draw facial features and clothing on the figure so it looks like a character from a book they are reading.

5. Have students bend the feet forward and fold the figure vertically so it can stand on its own.

6. Instruct students to write information about the character on the back of the card, such as personality traits, a description of the problem the character faces, the difference between the main character and a minor character, the importance of a character's actions, and so on.

7. Line the character cards along a shelf or countertop.

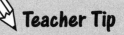 **Cross-Curriculum**

Invite students to work together to create a three-dimensional scene depicting the first Thanksgiving or some other historic event. Encourage students to write a few sentences on the back of each character card describing that person's point of view about this historic event.

Teacher Tip

Invite students to create an autobiographical timeline by constructing a character card of themselves for each year they've lived, each card getting a little taller than the previous one. Ask students to write about an important event from each year on the backs of the cards.

Setting the Scene

Materials
- large index cards
- scissors
- colored pencils or markers

Purpose
Students create easels and drawings that depict the major setting of a story they are reading.

Directions

1. Have students fold a large index card in half.

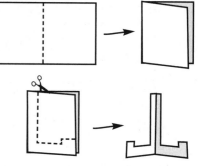

2. Instruct them to cut away an L-shaped portion of the card to create an easel.

3. On the lined side of a second index card, have students brainstorm a list of nouns that could be found in the setting of a story they are reading.

4. Have students draw a picture of the setting (horizontally or vertically) on the blank side of the card, using the nouns to help them be more detailed.

5. Stand the pictures in the easels. Display along a counter or shelf.

Teacher Tip
Tie this activity into your language arts curriculum. If you are studying adjectives, you could ask students to list adjectives that describe the setting rather than nouns that can be found in the setting.

Cross-Curriculum
In science class, read nonfiction books about different habitats. Encourage students to create easels featuring pictures of various habitats.

O.W.L.S.

Linking Books to Life Experiences
- Graphic Organizer -
Fiction/Nonfiction

Materials

- O.W.L.S. graphic organizers (pages 72–73)

Purpose

Students make connections between characters or simple events in a literary work and people or events in their lives.

Directions

1. After reading each chapter of a class book, or after reading a picture book, ask students to sit in a circle in an open area of your classroom where everyone can see one another.

2. Introduce the concept of O.W.L.S., which asks students to discuss things they *observed* in the chapter, things they *wondered* about as they read, ways they could *link* the story to their own lives, and ways in which their *senses* (sight, hearing, taste, smell, touch) were aroused. As students become more accustomed to this style of discussing books, they will be more likely to make the connections to their own life experiences while they are reading.

3. After several whole-class discussions, students will be able to complete the graphic organizers more easily. Pass out copies of the two O.W.L.S. graphic organizers to students, and have them fill them out based on their reaction to the last chapter or story they read. Then tape the two pages together.

Teacher Tip

Introduce this reading strategy while teaching a unit on owls! There are many fiction and nonfiction books that use owls as major and supporting characters, such as:
- *Baby Owl* by Aubrey Lang (Fitzhenry and Whiteside Limited, 2004)
- *Barn Owl* by Sally Tagholm (Kingfisher, 2003)
- *Owl at Home* by Arnold Lobel (HarperTrophy, 1982)
- *Owl Moon* by Jane Yolen (Philomel, 1987)
- *Snow Moon* by Nicholas Brunelle (Viking Juvenile, 2005)

Name _____ Date _____

O.W.L.S. Graphic Organizer

What did you **observe** as you read?

What did you **wonder** about as you read?

Name _____ Date _____

O.W.L.S. Graphic Organizer

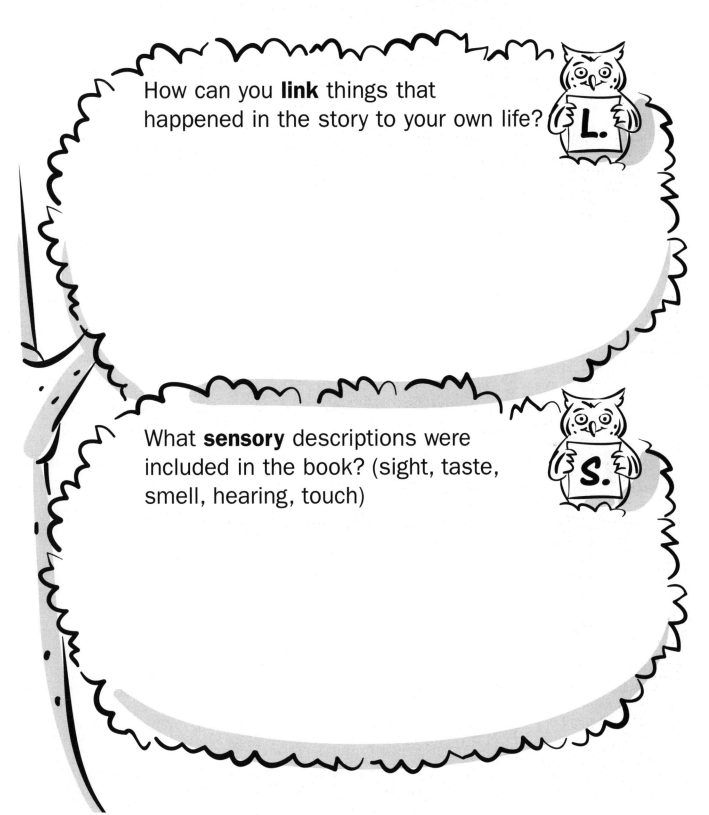

How can you **link** things that happened in the story to your own life? **L.**

What **sensory** descriptions were included in the book? (sight, taste, smell, hearing, touch) **S.**

Bookworms

Materials

- BOOKWORM templates (pages 75–76)
- colored pencils or markers
- scissors
- tape

Purpose

Students identify and sequence the main actions or events in a story they are reading.

Directions

1. Make copies of the BOOKWORM templates and pass them out to students.

2. Color and cut out the bookworm's head. Tape it to a wall in your classroom or in the hall.

3. As you read a story in class, assign a page or short section of the book to each student.

4. Have students reread their assigned section and write a sentence that details the main action or event on the lines of one of the body segments.

5. Have students draw and color a picture of the main action or event in the space above the lines. They should also write the page number at the top of the segment and color the legs.

6. Finally, have students cut out their bookworm segment and bring it to class.

7. Put the segments in sequential order and tape them onto the wall to create a long bookworm. When you're done, you'll have a page-by-page visual record of the story.

Cross-Curriculum

Invite students to sequence key moments of a historical event. Simply change the word "page" to the word "date" on the bookworm template and make copies for students.

Bookworm Template 1

PAGE _____

Name _____ Date _____

Bookworm Template 2

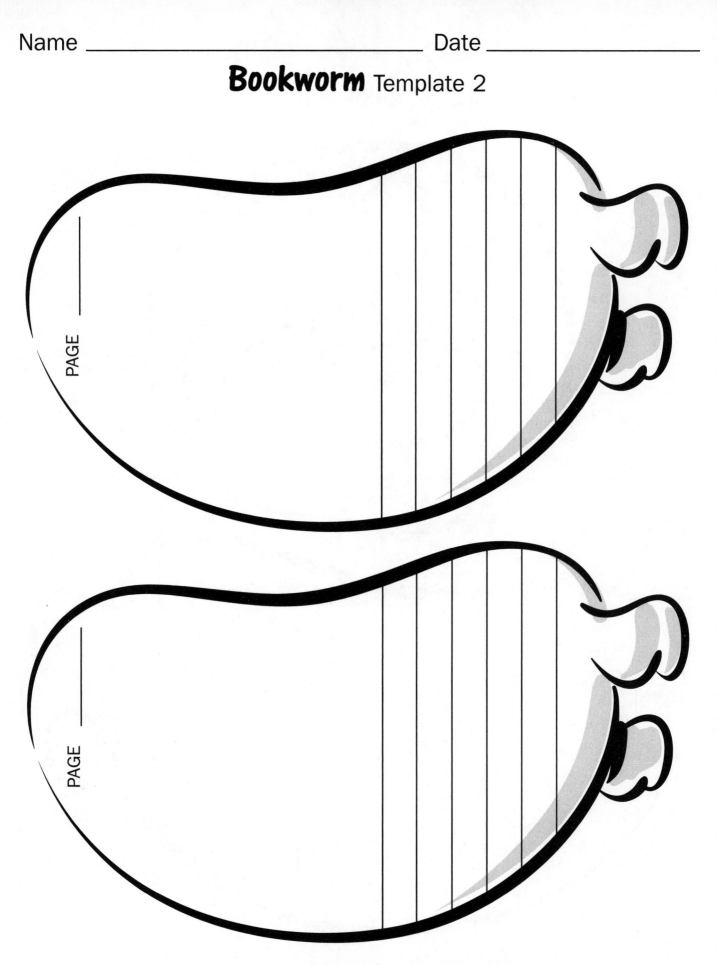

PAGE ____

PAGE ____

Reading an Article
- Graphic Organizer -
Nonfiction

Extra! Extra!

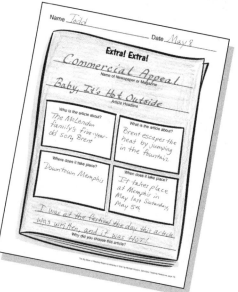

Materials

- EXTRA! EXTRA! graphic organizer (page 78)

Purpose

Students summarize and paraphrase information from a newspaper or magazine article.

Directions

1. Each day help a different student find an age-appropriate newspaper or magazine article that interests him or her. Tell the student to clip out the article, fill out the EXTRA! EXTRA! graphic organizer, and prepare to discuss the article in front of the class. The presenter should be sure to touch on the 5 Ws (who, what, where, when, and why).

2. After the oral presentation, allow the class to ask questions. This is a great way to generate discussions about what is happening in the world.

3. Display the articles and the graphic organizers on a bulletin board that reads, EXTRA! EXTRA!

Cross-Curriculum

Encourage students to find magazines that focus on specific subjects. You might try *Ranger Rick, Dragonfly, Appleseeds, Weekly Reader,* and others.

Name _____ Date _____

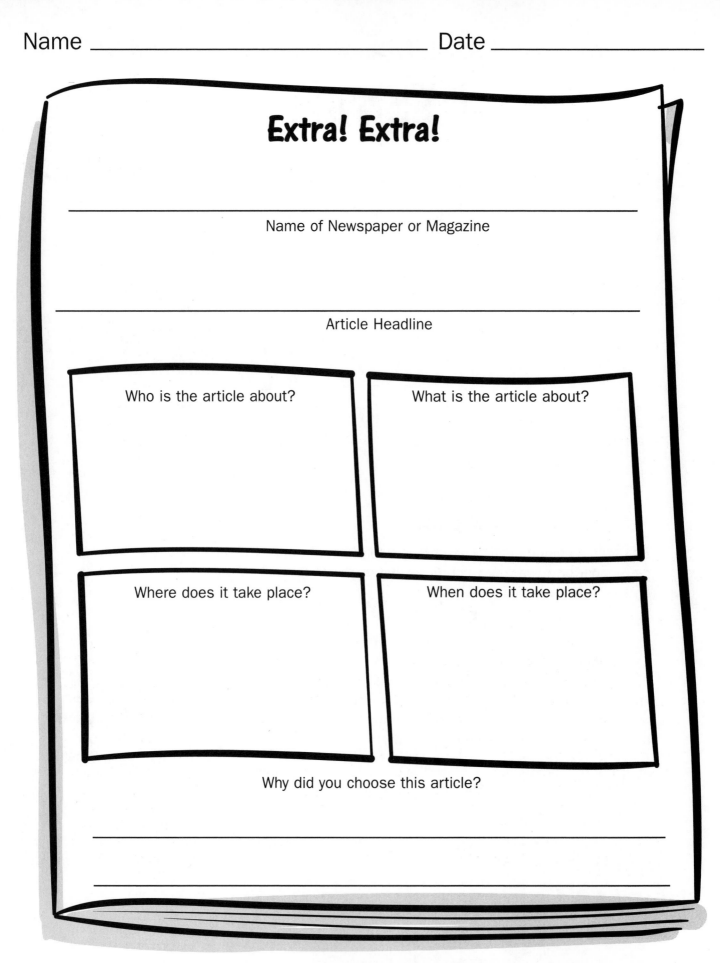

Extra! Extra!

_____

Name of Newspaper or Magazine

_____

Article Headline

Who is the article about?	What is the article about?

Where does it take place?	When does it take place?

Why did you choose this article?

_____

_____

You Don't Say!

Looking at
Dialogue
- Graphic Organizer -
Fiction

Name _Laura_   Date _October 13_

You Don't Say!
Charlotte's Web
Book Title
Wilbur
Character's Name

What does the character say?

Templeton, I will make you a solemn promise. Get Charlotte's egg sac for me, and from now on I will let you eat first, when Lurvy slops me. I will let you have your choice of everything and I won't touch a thing until you're through.

What does this quotation reveal about the character?

This quotation proves how much Wilbur loves Charlotte. It also proves that he is responsible. Charlotte died and Wilbur will do anything possible to make sure Charlotte's children are safe. Wilbur has become a true friend.

Materials

- YOU DON'T SAY! graphic organizer (page 80)

Purpose

Students examine how dialogue helps reveal character.

Directions

1. Discuss with the class the idea that character is often revealed through dialogue. What a person says and how he acts reveals information about his character. Is what she says truthful or false? Serious or funny? What does the character say about himself? What does the character say about others? Do the character's actions support her words?

2. Pass out a copy of the graphic organizer to each student.

3. Have students find a line of dialogue in the story that reveals character. Ask them to write it in the quote balloon on the graphic organizer.

4. Then ask students to describe what the character's words reveal about him or her.

Cross-Curriculum

Look on the Internet for sites that list quotations by famous people, sorted by theme, for quotations related to a topic you're studying. Ask students to use the graphic organizer to explain the meaning of the quotation.

Name _____ Date _____

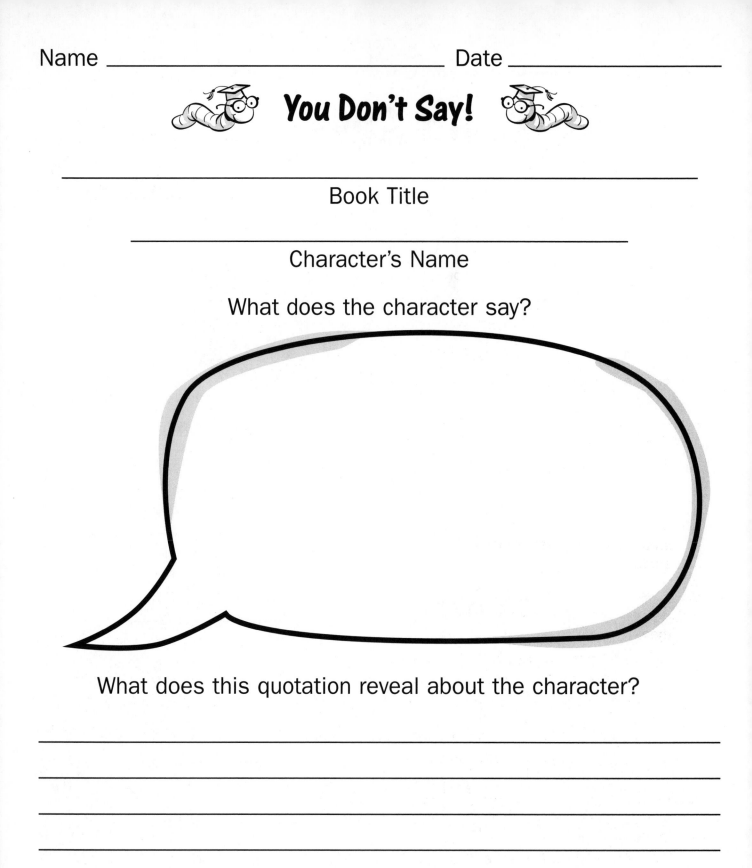

You Don't Say!

Book Title

_____

Character's Name

What does the character say?

What does this quotation reveal about the character?

_____

_____

_____

_____

_____

Quick and Easy Puppets

Materials

- 8½- by 11-inch white copier paper
- tape
- colored pencils or markers

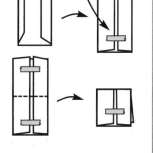

Purpose

Students retell a story using handmade puppets.

Directions

1. Give each student a sheet of white copier paper.

2. Instruct them to place it vertically in front of them and fold the two sides inward so they meet in the center. Have students crease the two folds.

3. Have students stick tape across the top and bottom of the two flaps to hold them together.

4. Instruct students to fold the paper in half so the flaps are on the outer side. Have them crease this fold.

5. Ask student to fold the ends toward the crease they just made. The flaps should be on the inside of these folds.

6. Show students how to slip their thumb and little finger into the lower opening and their middle three fingers into the upper opening to create a moving mouth.

7. Have students decorate the puppet so it looks like a character from a book they are reading.

8. Pair up students (or put them in groups of three or more) and have them use their puppets to retell a scene or chapter from a book they are reading. Tell them to focus on using dialogue to help tell the story.

tape

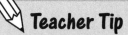

Teacher Tip

Explain to students that dialogue moves a story forward and reveals information about the character who is speaking. Tell students to think about *how* characters speak and how they express themselves. For example, how would two enemies say hello to each other? What words would they use? What feeling would be behind the words? How would two best friends say hello? Two strangers? A simple hello changes significantly depending on who the characters are and what their relationship is.

Figurative
Language
- Graphic Organizer -
Fiction

The Search Is On

The Search Is On

Name _Keislu_   Date _November 2_

Find two examples of _____Simile_____
Write them in the binoculars with the page numbers.

Page _38_

Paul Bunyan's axe
split the trees like
swift bolts of lightning.

Page _44_

To his surprise the
ox was as blue as a
deep night sky and as
large as a mighty pine.

Materials

- THE SEARCH IS ON graphic organizer (page 84)

Purpose

Students explore ways in which figurative language is used in literary texts.

Directions

1. Look over the list on page 83 and choose a figure of speech. Discuss its meaning with the class, and share examples.

2. Make a copy of THE SEARCH IS ON graphic organizer. Write the figure of speech on the top line. Make copies and give one to each student.

3. Instruct students to look for examples of the figure of speech in a book they're reading. In each lens of the binoculars, have students write the full sentence with the figure of speech and the page number.

Teacher Tip

Encourage students to develop an ear for figurative language. After you've reviewed a particular figure of speech, conduct a read aloud and invite students to raise their hand whenever they hear an example.

Figurative Language

Simile

a comparison between two dissimilar things using like *or* as

Example: The fog hugged the mountain like a warm coat.

Alliteration

the repetition of the initial sound in adjacent words or syllables

Example: Suddenly, winter winds whirled in from the west, towing white, woolly clouds in their wake.

Metaphor

a direct comparison between two dissimilar things that does not use the words like *or* as

Example: The clouds were a wagon train lumbering across the January sky.

Onomatopoeia

the use of a word whose sound suggests its meaning

Example: *Whoosh!* the winds cried loudly. *Rumble!* the clouds growled in reply.

Assonance

the repetition of vowel sounds within a series of words

Example: The downy clouds surrounded the mountain and covered it with powdery snow.

Personification

to show something that is not human behaving in a human way

Example: The mountain became king, standing proudly in his royal white robes, surveying the realm around him.

Name _____

The Search Is On

Find two examples of _____ .
Write them in the binoculars with the page numbers.

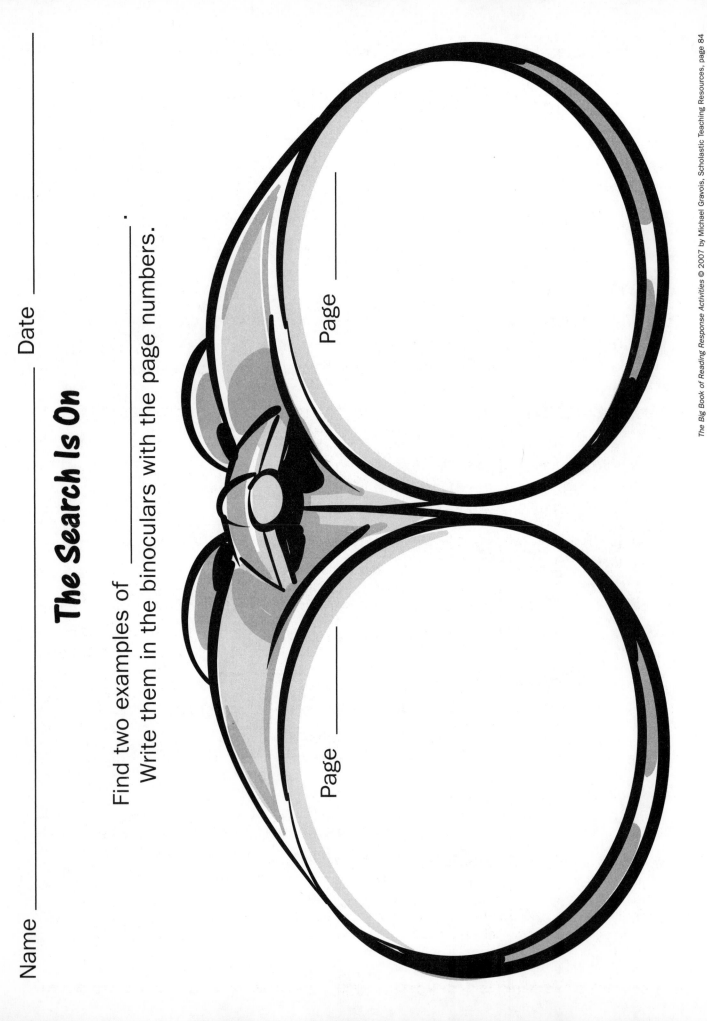

Page ____

Page ____

Main Idea Ship

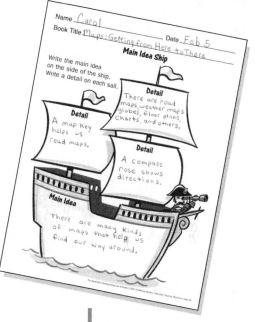

Materials

- MAIN IDEA SHIP graphic organizer (page 86)

Purpose

Students find the main idea and supporting details of a particular topic.

Directions

1. Pass out a copy of the MAIN IDEA SHIP graphic organizer to each student.

2. Explain the organizing principles of main idea and details. For example, "Man landed on the moon" might be the main idea of a unit on space travel. "Neil Armstrong was the first person to walk on the moon" and "The first moon landing was in 1969" would be details.

3. For this activity, have students pick a topic to research or invite them to respond to a section in a textbook or nonfiction book.

4. Have students write a sentence that explains the book's main idea on the side of the ship.

5. On the sails, have them write three important details they have gathered from their research.

Cross-Curriculum

This graphic organizer lends itself to all curricular topics. Invite students to research famous people, countries, rules of grammar, animals, simple machines, space voyages, and so on. Encourage them to use the information they collected as resource material for completing another project in this book.

Name _____ Date _____

Book Title _____

Main Idea Ship

Write the main idea
on the side of the ship.
Write a detail on each sail.

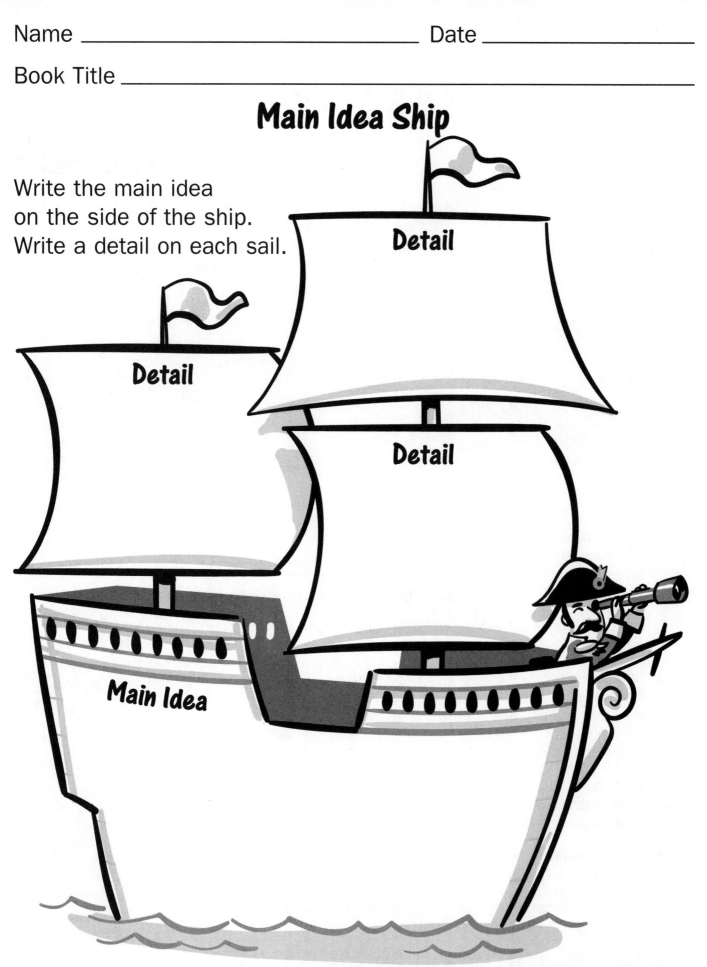

Detail

Detail

Detail

Main Idea

Wanted Posters

Describing Antagonists
- Activity -
Fiction/Nonfiction

Materials

- WANTED POSTER template (page 88)
- colored pencils or markers

Purpose

Students create posters that identify and describe the antagonist in a story they are reading.

Directions

1. Pass out a copy of the WANTED POSTER template to each student.

2. Explain that an antagonist is the adversary of the hero (or protagonist) of a story.

3. Challenge students to create a Wild West–style "wanted" poster that highlights the misdeeds of the antagonist of a story they are reading. In the box at the top of the page, invite students to draw and color a picture of the antagonist.

4. Have students write a paragraph describing who the antagonist is and what he or she is wanted for or what he or she has done wrong.

Cross-Curriculum

In health class, invite students to draw pictures of things that are antagonistic to good health—such as germs, junk food, and poor hygiene—and describe why these things are unhealthy.

Name _____ Date _____

Book Title _____

Draw a picture of the antagonist. Write about why he or she is wanted.

WANTED

_____
_____
_____
_____
_____
_____

Words for the Wise

Learning
Vocabulary
- Graphic Organizer -
Fiction/Nonfiction

Materials

- WORDS FOR THE WISE graphic organizer (page 90)
- dictionary
- thesaurus

Purpose

Students learn the meanings of new vocabulary words.

Directions

1. Pass out of a copy of the WORDS FOR THE WISE graphic organizer to each student.

2. Instruct students to write a vocabulary word from a book they are reading in the shaded rectangle.

3. Have students look up the word's definition and write it in their own words in the space provided.

4. Tell students to write a few synonyms for the word in the space provided. Encourage them to use a thesaurus.

5. In the lower left section, have students write a sentence that uses the vocabulary word meaningfully.

6. Finally, have students draw a picture of the word. If the word is not a concrete noun, they may need to find a way to illustrate the concept (especially if the word is a feeling, adjective, or idea).

Teacher Tip

Copy the WORDS FOR THE WISE graphic organizer on both sides of three-hole copier paper so students can create a vocabulary journal. Encourage them to use a three-ring binder or pocket folder to store all the vocabulary words they learn throughout the year.

Name _____ Date _____

Words for the Wise

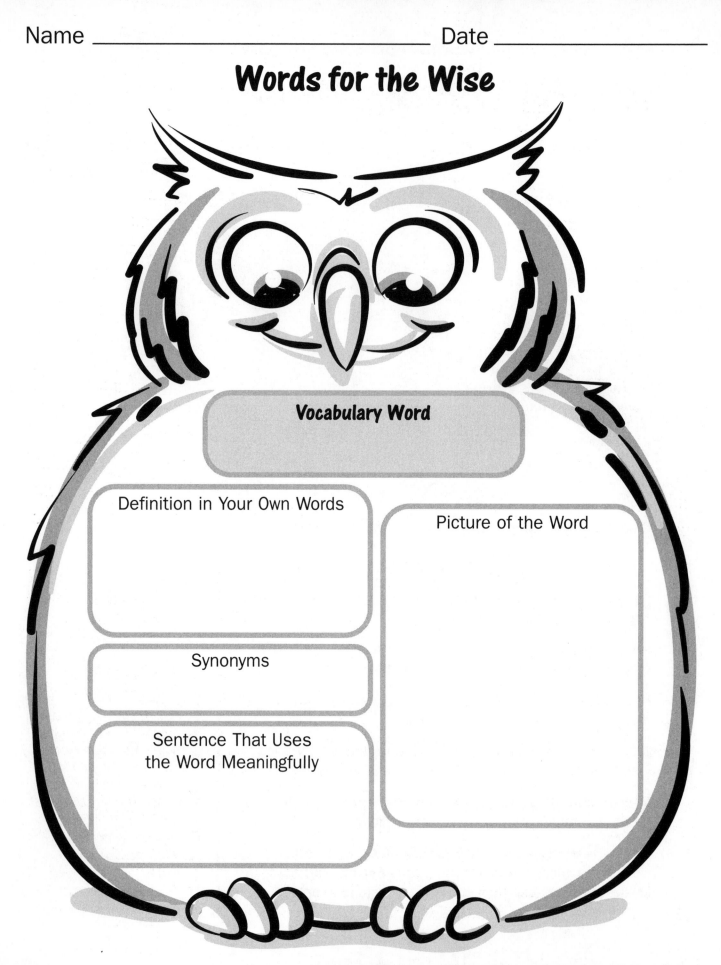

Vocabulary Word

Definition in Your Own Words

Picture of the Word

Synonyms

Sentence That Uses
the Word Meaningfully

Roll-a-Word

Vocabulary Game
- Activity -
Fiction/Nonfiction

Give an antonym for the vocabulary word.

Spell the vocabulary word.

Define the vocabulary word.

Materials

- ROLL-A-WORD CUBE template (page 92)
- colored pencils or markers
- scissors
- glue

Purpose

Students play a word game to learn the meanings of new vocabulary words.

Directions

1. Make a copy of the ROLL-A-WORD CUBE template, and follow steps 2 through 5 to create the cube.

2. To make the cube more vibrant, color the six large sections different colors.

3. Cut out the cube along the solid lines.

4. Fold along the dotted lines so it forms a cube.

5. Glue each of the tabs behind the panel it meets.

6. Have students sit in a circle. Choose a volunteer to start the game.

7. Select a vocabulary word from a book the students are reading and then roll the cube. Instruct the student to answer the question that appears on the top side of the cube.

Teacher Tip

Use the Roll-a-Word game as a review for an upcoming vocabulary test. Divide the class into two teams. Alternate between teams—picking a vocabulary word, rolling the cube, and having a team member answer the question. Each correct answer earns a point for the team. The team with the most points at the end of the game wins.

Roll-a-Word Cube

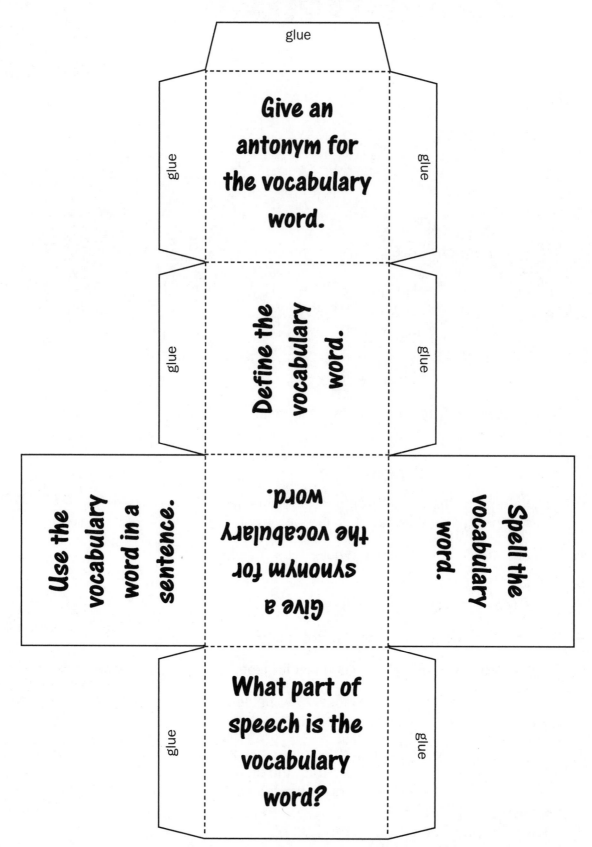

glue

glue

Give an antonym for the vocabulary word.

glue

glue

Define the vocabulary word.

glue

Use the vocabulary word in a sentence.

Give a synonym for the vocabulary word.

Spell the vocabulary word.

glue

What part of speech is the vocabulary word?

glue

Conference Wheel

Classroom
Management
- Activity -
Fiction/Nonfiction

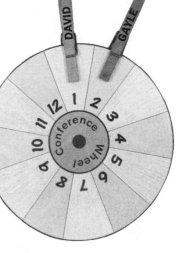

Materials

- CONFERENCE WHEEL template (page 94)
- glue stick
- posterboard or cardboard
- clothespins
- marker
- string

Purpose

This conference wheel will help you manage the reading classroom by providing a quick reference of the names of students who want to conference with you.

Directions

1. Glue a copy of the CONFERENCE WHEEL template to a piece of posterboard or cardboard.

2. Cut out the wheel.

3. Use a marker to write each student's name on a clothespin.

4. Hang the clothespins on a length of string that spans a bulletin board or wall.

5. When students are in the middle of a reading or writing assignment and they need to conference with you, have them take their clothespin and clip it to the next available slot on the conference wheel. Display the wheel on a wall near the conference area for easy reference.

6. When you are ready to meet with the next student, call him or her to the conference area. Call up each student sequentially. This prevents continual interruptions when speaking with individual students.

7. Hand students their clothespin when the conference has ended so they can clip it back onto the string.

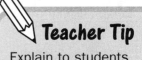

Teacher Tip

Explain to students that if they have a question and they've put their name on the conference wheel, they should continue working on other aspects of their assignment while they are waiting their turn.

Conference Wheel Template

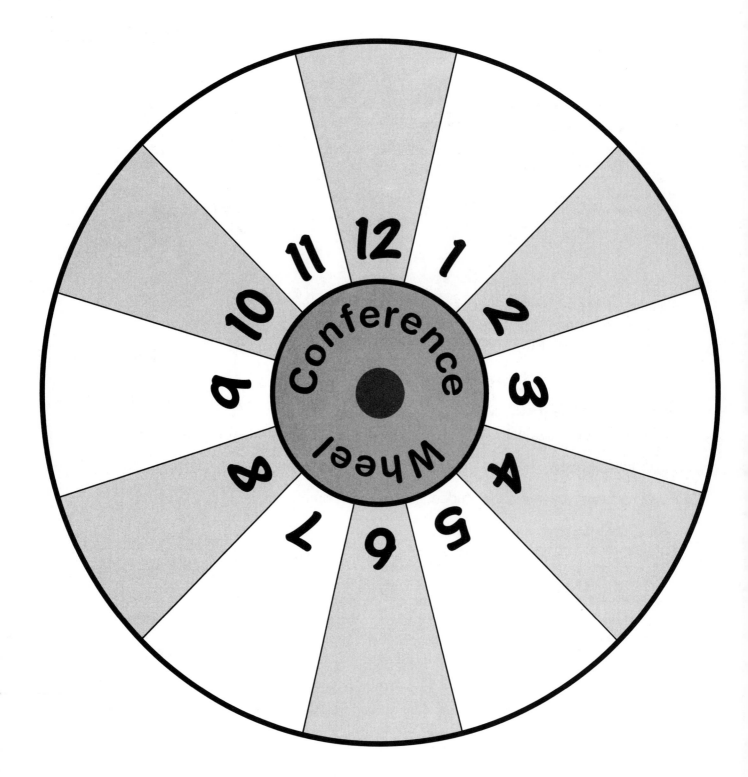

30-20-10 Talks

Reading
Comprehension
- Activity -
Fiction/Nonfiction

Purpose

Students use listening and speaking skills to retell a story and improve their reading comprehension.

Directions

1. Have students read a chapter silently to themselves, aloud in groups, or as a whole class.

2. Divide the class into pairs of reading partners, and have them sit next to each other.

3. After reading the chapter, have one reading partner (student A) begin retelling the chapter to the second reading partner (student B) for 30 seconds.

4. When you call "switch," student B begins retelling the chapter—from the point where student A stopped—for another 30 seconds.

5. Call "switch" again. Student A continues for 20 seconds. When you call "switch" again, student B continues for 20 seconds.

6. Finally, each student has 10 seconds to finish retelling the chapter.

Teacher Tip

Vary the 30-20-10 talks by asking pairs to discuss a favorite scene, passage, or quotation. Or ask the pairs to discuss something they had a difficult time understanding or an issue that interested them.

Problem and
Solution
- Creative Dramatics -
Fiction

Role-Playing

Purpose

Students improvise scenes to examine the concepts of problem and solution in a literary text.

Directions

1. Have students identify the major problem in a book the class is reading. Then divide the class into small groups. The groups should have as many members as there are main characters in the book.

2. Ask the groups to discuss the problem in the story and to devise a scene that offers a solution to the problem. Each student should play a different character from the book.

3. Invite the groups, one at a time, to come to the front of the class and improvise the scene. The scene should introduce the problem and continue until the solution has been presented.

4. After all the groups have had a chance to perform, discuss the different solutions that the groups developed. Then continue reading the story to see how the author solved the problem.

Soundscapes

Creating Atmosphere
- Creative Dramatics -
Fiction/Nonfiction

Purpose

Students create sound effects to examine the use of atmosphere and mood in a story's setting.

Directions

1. Tell your class that a *landscape* uses images to create a picture, but a *soundscape* uses sounds.

2. Divide the class into groups of four or five.

3. Whisper the name of a different scene from a book you're reading to each group.

4. Tell students that they can use their feet, hands, mouths, or materials found around the classroom to create sounds that one might hear in the given environment, but they can not use any words. For example, if the scene took place during a walk in the woods at night, students might create the sounds of owls hooting, crickets chirping, wolves howling, wind blowing, footsteps falling, and leaves rustling. Each student can make more than one sound.

5. Tell students from other groups to turn away from the group performing, so only the sounds cue them into the atmosphere, not the performers' movements. Challenge the other groups to identify the setting.

6. Once a setting has been identified, ask the other groups if they have suggestions for additional sounds that could have been used to create the atmosphere.

Teacher Tip

Aural learning is one of the multiple intelligences that is rarely used, aside from listening to a speaker. This activity challenges students to think aurally and helps them to better understand the importance that atmosphere plays in a story.

Cross-Curriculum

Ask students to write a script for a radio play and record it on a tape recorder. Invite students to think of ways that soundscapes could be used to create atmosphere. Imagine the background sounds that would be heard as the Pilgrims stepped off the *Mayflower* or if the class took a trip to the rain forest.

Book-of-the-Week Bulletin Board

Materials

- BOOK-OF-THE-WEEK BOOK REPORT template (page 100)
- BOOK-OF-THE-WEEK REPORT COVER template (page 101)
- stapler
- colored pencils or markers

Purpose

Students create a bulletin board and contribute to a class discussion about favorite books to reinforce the purpose of reading for pleasure.

Directions

1. At the end of each week discuss all the books you read in class. Either choose a featured book yourself or allow the students to choose the book they enjoyed most.

2. Pass out a copy of the BOOK-OF-THE-WEEK BOOK REPORT template to each student.

3. Ask students to rate the book (out of five stars), and have them color in that number of stars at the top of the page. (They can color in half stars as well.)

4. Below the stars, have students write a paragraph describing what they liked about the book and draw a picture of a favorite scene.

Cross-Curriculum

Help students understand the concept of averaging numbers by having them work in pairs to find the average number of stars that each week's featured book receives.

5. Collect the forms and add up the number of stars given to the book. Divide that total by the number of students who reviewed the book to get the average number of stars the book received.

6. Choose a different student each week to create a cover for the class book report, and give that student a copy of the BOOK-OF-THE-WEEK REPORT COVER template.

7. Show the student how to use the template to create a book cover that includes the title, the author's name, and an illustration. At the top of the form, have the student fill in the average number of stars the book received.

8. Collect the report cover and all the reports and staple them together.

9. Display the class book report on a bulletin board under a banner that reads, BOOK-OF-THE-WEEK. Write the date the report was written on a strip of paper and display it above the report.

10. Each week, add another book to the bulletin board to create a year-long display to remind students of all the books they've read throughout the year.

Teacher Tip

Rather than creating one large bulletin board that displays all the books-of-the-week that have been read throughout the year, create a smaller display that features only the current book-of-the-week.

Name _____ Date _____

Title _____

Author _____

Book-of-the-Week Book Report

Rate the book by coloring the number of stars you think
the book should receive. Draw a picture of your favorite scene.
Write a paragraph describing what you liked about the book.

_____

_____

_____

_____

_____

Book-of-the-Week

(Average Number of Stars)

Somebody/Wanted/But/So/Then

Name _Ali_   Date _October 30_

SWBST Graphic Organizer

Somebody
(Character)

The Grand Witch

Wanted to eliminate all children

Wanted
(Goal)

but a boy discovered her plan

But
(Conflict)

So she turned him into a mouse

So
(Resolution)

The Witches
by
Roald Dahl
Title of Book

then he fed her the potion and she became a mouse

Then
(Conclusion)

Materials

- SWBST graphic organizer (page 103)

Purpose

Students identify the major plot points of a story.

Directions

1. The Somebody/Wanted/But/So/Then (SWBST) reading strategy allows you to evaluate a student's understanding of the main elements of a story by challenging them to retell the story in a few simple sentences.

2. Discuss this strategy with the class to help them create a statement that identifies a character (*somebody*), explains his or her goal (*wanted*), describes a conflict that impedes his or her actions (*but*), recognizes the resolution to the conflict (*so*), and recounts the outcome of these events (*then*).

3. Use a familiar story to illustrate this, such as, "Cinderella wanted to go to the ball, but she doesn't have a dress; so her fairy godmother creates one for her; then she meets her Prince Charming." Here's another example from the same story: "The prince wanted to marry Cinderella, but she runs away; so he tries to find a woman who fits the glass slipper she left behind; then they live happily ever after."

4. Tell the students that SWBST statements can be written to identify the main plot as well as subplots; they can describe major and minor characters; or they can identify the main ideas of each chapter.

5. Pass out a copy of the SWBST graphic organizer to each student.

6. Have students write a word or phrase on each of the fingers of the graphic organizer to identify the SWBST elements of a story they've read.

Teacher Tip

The SWBST reading strategy can be used to check comprehension while students are reading—on a chapter-by-chapter or character-by-character basis. This strategy also lends itself to postreading activities that help students summarize the main idea of the story.

Name _____

Date _____

SWBST Graphic Organizer

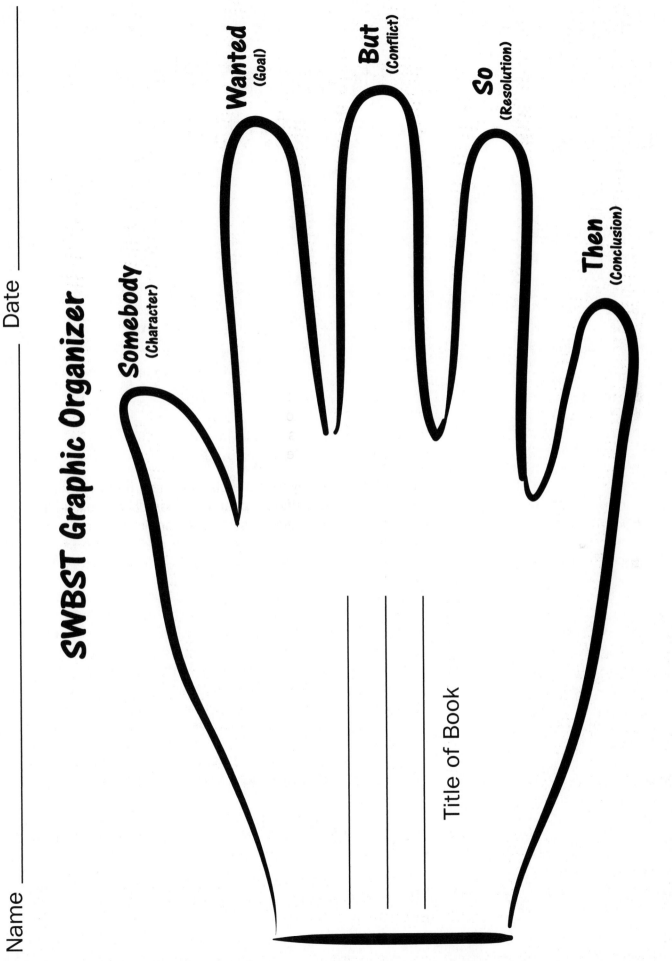

Somebody
(Character)

Wanted
(Goal)

But
(Conflict)

So
(Resolution)

Then
(Conclusion)

Title of Book

Point of View
- Activity -
Fiction/Nonfiction

Point of View Stationery

Dear Strega Nona,
I'm sorry I touched your magic pasta pot after you told me not to. I wanted to show off for the townspeople. I sure learned my lesson, and I promise to listen in the future.
Sincerely,
Big Anthony

Materials

- writing paper
- colored pencils and markers
- glue

Purpose

Students write a letter in the voice of a specific character to develop an understanding of the importance of point of view in a literary text.

Directions

1. Give each student a sheet of writing paper.

2. Discuss the meaning of *point of view*. Mention that a story might change depending on the point of view of the narrator. Describe how a disagreement on the playground has two different sides. Perhaps read a story like *The True Story of the Three Little Pigs* by Jon Scieszka to show how a story can change depending on who's telling it.

3. Instruct students to design a sheet of personalized stationery for a character from a book they've read. Have students create a border around the paper that reflects the character. For example, the stationery for the Hardy Boys could have a border of magnifying glasses, or the stationery for Tinkerbell could feature magic wands.

4. Have students write a letter that describes an event from the story as told from that character's point of view.

Character Sensory Charts

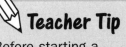

Character Study
- Graphic Organizer -
Fiction

Materials

- Five SENSES CHART (page 106)
- crayons
- colored pencils or markers

Purpose

Students examine the effects a story's setting has on the characters in the story.

Directions

1. Pass out a copy of the FIVE SENSES CHART to each student.

2. Ask students to think about a scene from a book they've read and a character who appeared in that scene.

3. Instruct students to use colored pencils or crayons to draw the character in the space on the left side of the chart. Have them write the character's name under the figure.

4. Tell students to brainstorm all the things the character would see in the scene's environment and list them on the chart next to the word *See*. Encourage students to reread the text to find support for their answers.

5. Have students brainstorm all the things the character would hear, smell, taste, and touch, listing them on the chart as well. Thinking about the things a character senses makes students look beyond the written word and step into the shoes of the character.

6. Discuss the word choices students made. Compare how the sensations a character experiences change from scene to scene depending on the situation and circumstances. Discuss the ways in which different environments affect your students' senses, and how that in turn can affect their attitude and disposition.

Teacher Tip

Before starting a creative writing assignment, encourage students to fill out a sensory chart for their main character. This will help students use richer language in their writing and create a more fully developed character.

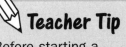

Name _____

Date _____

Book Title _____

Five Senses Chart

Think about a scene from the book. What does the character in that scene see? Hear? Smell? Taste? Touch? Write your answers in the chart below. Draw a picture of the character on the left.

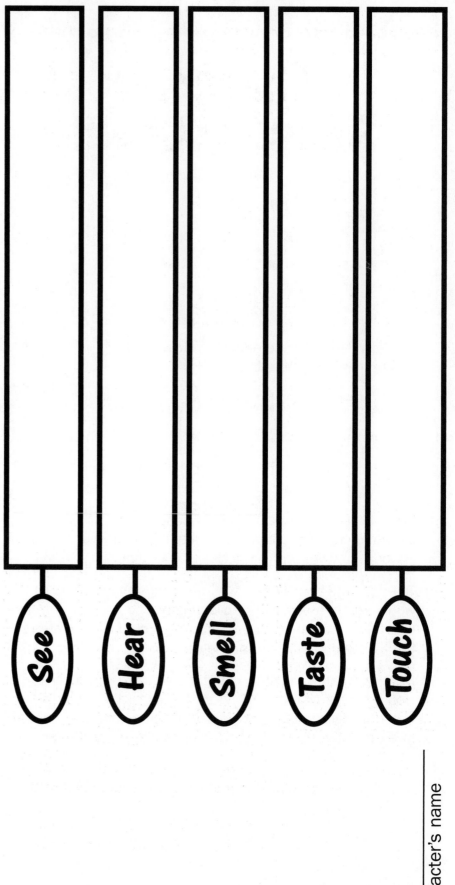

See

Hear

Smell

Taste

Touch

_____
character's name

Do/Learn/Feel Circle Books

Character
Book Reports
- Activity -
Fiction

4. Draw a picture of the character in an important scene from the story.

Materials

- CIRCLE BOOK TEMPLATES 1–4 (pages 109–112)
- different colored copier paper
- colored pencils or markers
- scissors
- glue sticks
- string
- thread
- paper clips

Purpose

Students examine elements of character development in literary works by describing things characters did, how they felt, and what they learned over the course of the story.

Directions

1. Copy templates 1–3 on different colored paper. Copy template 4 on white paper. Give each student a copy of each of the four templates.

2. On template 1, invite students to write a paragraph describing the major things a character did in the story.

3. On template 2, have students write a paragraph describing something the character learned over the course of the story.

4. On template 3, instruct students to write a paragraph describing how the character felt or how the character's feelings changed throughout the book.

5. On template 4, have students draw a picture of the character in a major scene from the book.

✳ Cross-Curriculum

Do/Learn/Feel responses can be used across the curriculum to track students' specific learning experiences. For example, have students describe what they did, what they learned, and how they felt about a science experiment they conducted, a field trip the class took, or a play the class staged.

6. After students have finished the four pages, instruct them to fold the pages in half along the vertical dashed lines and cut out the circles.

7. Have students glue the back right side of template 1 to the back left side of template 2.

8. Instruct students to glue the back right side of template 2 to the back left side of template 3. Repeat with templates 3 and 4.

9. To complete the circle books, have students glue the back right side of template 4 to the back left side of template 1.

10. Hang a string high across your classroom. Tie varying lengths of of thread from the string. Tie a paper clip to the end of each piece of thread and hang the circle books from the paper clips. When a breeze blows past the circle books, they will spin and create a vibrant display of the students' work.

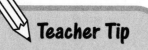

Teacher Tip

Circle books can be made from any symmetrically cut piece of paper. Think of a shape that relates to your curriculum—cloud books for a unit on weather, heart books for the human body, or flower books for plant life.

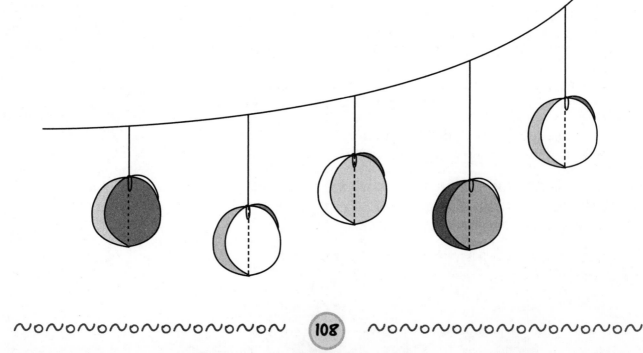

Name _____ Date _____

Circle Book Template 1

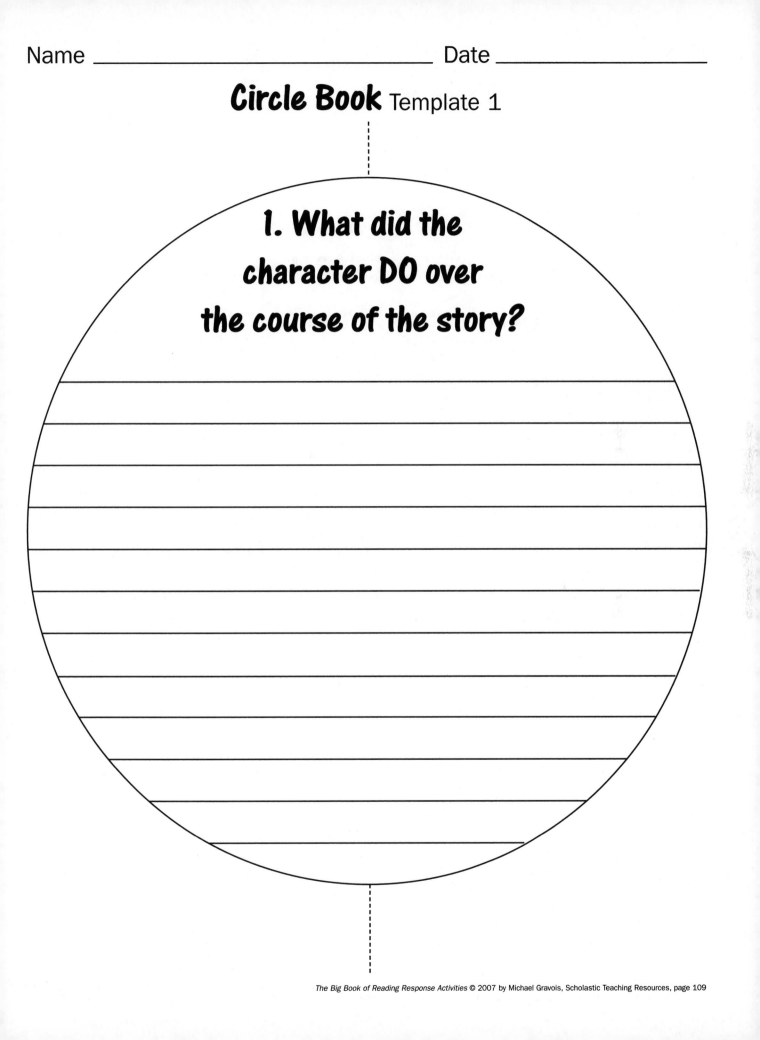

1. What did the
character DO over
the course of the story?

Name _____ Date _____

Circle Book Template 2

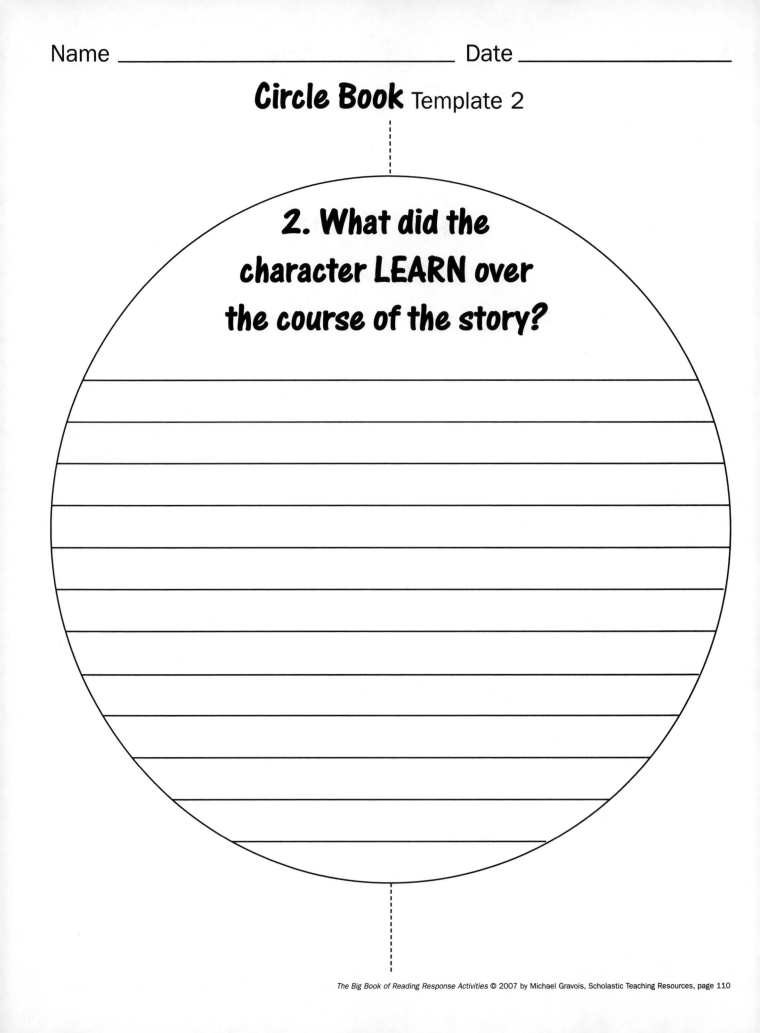

2. What did the character LEARN over the course of the story?

Name _____ Date _____

Circle Book Template 3

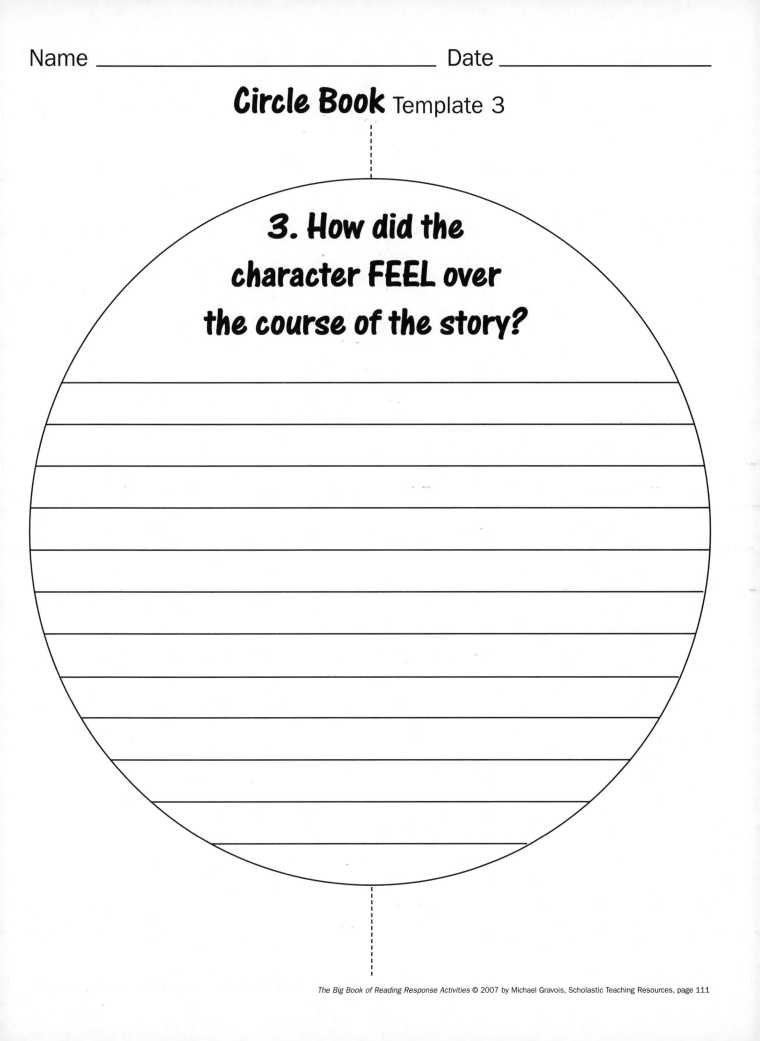

3. How did the character FEEL over the course of the story?

Name _____ Date _____

Circle Book Template 4

4. Draw a picture
of the character in an
important scene from the story.

Key Events Timeline

Sequencing With Timelines
- Bulletin Board -
Fiction/Nonfiction

Materials

- white and black construction paper
- scissors
- colored pencils or markers
- tape

Purpose

Students sequence key events in a story's plot.

Directions

1. Cut sheets of 8½- by 11-inch white construction paper in half lengthwise to make two rectangles that measure 4¼ by 11 inches. You'll need one rectangle for each student in your class.

2. Cut sheets of black construction paper into rectangles that measure 2 by 5 inches and set aside.

3. Give each student one of the white rectangles. Ask students to place it vertically in front of them. Tell them each to illustrate a different key event from a class novel, a person's life, a historical period, and so on. At the bottom of the rectangle, have students write a few sentences describing the scene. On nonfiction timelines, instruct students to write the date of the event depicted.

4. Hang the "keys" in chronological order on a bulletin board.

5. To complete the keyboard, tape black keys between the white keys.

6. Hang a banner above the keyboard that reads, KEY EVENTS IN _____ , filling in the context.

Teacher Tip

Read the biography of a great composer, singer, or musician and have students create a musical timeline of the person's life. Have each student create a piano key that illustrates an important event or significant accomplishment.

Sequencing
Key Plot Points
- Activity -
Fiction

Key Events Key Chain

Materials
- KEY EVENTS template (page 115)
- colored pencils or markers
- scissors
- hole punch
- string or yarn

Teacher Tip

Discuss rules that lead to a successful classroom, behavior that leads to successful friendships, actions that lead to accomplishing goals, and other life lessons. Have each student illustrate and describe one of the traits you discussed. Create a "cover" key that reads KEYS TO SUCCESS. Add students' work to the key chain. Hang the key chain at the front of the classroom so you can refer to these important life lessons throughout the year.

Purpose
Students sequence key events in a story's plot.

Directions

1. Give each student four copies of the KEY EVENTS template.

2. On the head of one key, have students write "Key Events" at the top and their book title at the bottom. Instruct them to draw an illustration in the center and write the author's name and their name on the lines to the right.

3. On the heads of other three keys, have students illustrate key events from the story. Above each picture, instruct students to write the phrase "Key Event" followed by the number 1, 2, or 3 to correspond with the order of the events. Then have students write a sentence on each key describing the scenes they illustrated.

4. Punch a hole through the circle on each key and have students create a key chain out of a length of string or yarn.

5. Display the key chains on a bulletin board.

Key Events Template

First, Next, Then, Finally Books

Materials

- FIRST, NEXT, THEN, FINALLY template (page 117)
- scissors
- tape
- colored pencils or markers

Purpose

Students sequence the chain of events that led to a historical incident.

Directions

1. Pass out copies of the FIRST, NEXT, THEN, FINALLY template.

2. Instruct students to cut the template in half along the dashed line.

3. Tell them to lay the two halves side by side so the panels read "First," "Next," "Then," and "Finally," from left to right.

4. Tape the halves together into one long strip.

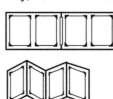

5. Show students how to accordion fold the four panels.

6. In the fourth frame, titled "Finally," have students draw a picture of a historical event they've read about in a textbook or other nonfiction book. Instruct them to write the title of the event on the lines below the illustration.

7. In the frames titled "First," "Next," and "Then," have students illustrate and describe three events that lead to the historical incident.

8. Have students close their book and design a cover.

Cross-Curriculum

Encourage students to use these books to write and illustrate the step-by-step directions for solving a math problem, to sequence major events from a story, or to explain key steps in a scientific experiment.

First

Next

Then

Finally

Finger Puppets

Materials

- white construction paper
- colored pencils or markers
- scissors
- tape
- rulers

Purpose

Students retell a story they read using finger puppets.

Directions

1. Have students cut out a 3$\frac{1}{2}$-inch square of construction paper for each finger puppet.

2. Ask students to fold the paper in half vertically to create a center line.

3. Have students draw the torso of their finger puppet using the center line as the line of symmetry. They should add details and color the character.

4. Instruct students to turn the paper over and draw a line one half inch from the bottom. They should fold the paper up along this line.

5. Show students how to cut along the top edge of the fold and around the outer edge of the character, leaving a folded band across the bottom. Here's a back view of the puppet.

6. Instruct students to curl the band toward them, tuck one side into the other, and secure it with tape.

7. Have students slip the puppets onto their fingers and use them to retell a story they've read.

Leveling Tip

Encourage interaction with younger grades by pairing your students with kindergartners. Have the older students tell a fairy tale to the younger children using finger puppets. Then have the kindergartners retell the story to their partners.

Teacher Tip

Create a puppet theater out of an old washing machine box that you can get from an appliance store. Cut a window, add curtains, and decorate the exterior. Students will have a blast performing stories for their friends.

Author! Author! Domino Books

Author
Study
- Activity -
Fiction/Nonfiction

Materials

- white legal paper (8½ by 14 inches)
- scissors
- tape
- colored pencils or markers
- picture books by the same author

Purpose

Students examine the effects an author's or illustrator's style has on the reader.

Directions

1. Read aloud a few books by the same author or illustrator. Discuss similarities and differences between the books. Challenge students to each read two or three books by the same author or illustrator.

2. Pass out a sheet of white legal paper to each student, and tell them to cut the sheet in half vertically so they end up with two long strips of paper.

4. Have students place the strips next to each other horizontally as shown and tape the edges, forming one long strip.

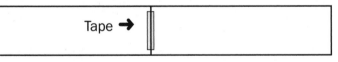

5. Show students how to fold this long strip in half three times. When they open it back up, the strip will be divided into eight panels, as shown below.

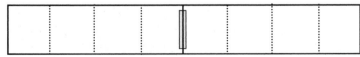

6. Tell them to fold the far right edge inward, creasing the paper along the first fold.

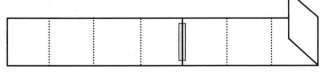

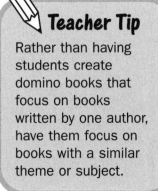 **Teacher Tip**

Rather than having students create domino books that focus on books written by one author, have them focus on books with a similar theme or subject.

7. Instruct students to continue folding the paper inward (a total of seven times), creasing along each fold.

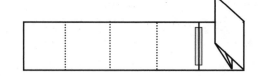

8. When they have finished the last fold, have students flip the domino book over. The top panel will serve as the cover. (This panel should open toward the left, like the cover of a book. The interior panels will "roll" out toward the right.)

9. On the cover, have students create a title, such as "Kyle's Domino Book About Eric Carle."

10. When students open the cover, it will reveal two panels.

   - On the left panel, have them write the author's name and a sentence describing why they chose that author.

   - On the right panel, have students write the titles of the books they read.

11. As students open each consecutive panel, they will reveal six more pairs of panels. On the left and right panels, have students include the following responses:

Pair #	Left Panel	Right Panel
2	Write the title of your favorite book by this author.	Why is this your favorite?
3	Write the illustrator's name.	Draw a picture from a book in the style of the illustrator.
4	Draw a picture of your favorite character.	Write five adjectives that describe this character.
5	Write a sentence from a book that you like.	What do you like about this sentence?
6	Write the word "Similarities."	Write a sentence describing similarities between the books.
7	Write the word "Differences."	Write a sentence describing differences between the books.

Teacher Tip

Turn a domino book on its side so the panels fall downward, like photos in a wallet. Have students create wallet photos that a character from a story might treasure. The photos could show family members and friends, important events from the story, and keepsakes the character might carry. Have students fold a piece of construction paper in half, glue the wallet photos inside, and trim off excess paper. Have them write a title on the cover, such as "This Wallet Belongs to Little Red Riding Hood."

I'm Your Number One Fan

Celebrating
Favorite Books
- Activity -
Fiction/Nonfiction

Materials

- I'M YOUR NUMBER ONE FAN template (page 122)
- colored pencils or markers
- scissors
- tape

Purpose

Students write fan letters to a favorite author.

Directions

1. Pass out copies of the I'M YOUR NUMBER ONE FAN template.

2. Have students cut out the fan shapes, leaving the tab attached.

3. On the back of the fan, instruct students to write a fan letter to the author of a favorite book explaining why they like the book so much.

4. There are four panels on the front of the fan. In the first panel, tell students to write their name, the name of their favorite book, and the author's name.

5. Have students draw a picture of their favorite scene in the second panel and a picture of their favorite character in the third panel. Remind them to include the character's name.

6. In the fourth panel, instruct students to write four words that describe how they felt while they were reading this book.

7. Show students how to accordion fold the four panels back and forth along the dashed lines to create a fan.

8. To display the fans, tape the tabs onto a bulletin board, allowing the fans to fall forward.

Leveling Tip

To make a longer fan book, glue the tab of one fan to the fourth panel of a second fan. This creates an eight-panel fan book and allows for more response space.

Teacher Tip

To create a tighter fan, have students double fold each panel.

I'm Your Number One Fan Template

tab

Cut out the fan.
Keep the tab attached.

Character Counts!

Comparing
Characters
- Graphic Organizer -
Fiction/Nonfiction

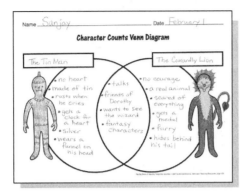

Materials

- CHARACTER COUNTS Venn diagram (page 124)
- colored pencils or markers

Purpose

Students examine the similarities and differences between two characters in a story.

Directions

1. Pass out a copy of the CHARACTER COUNTS VENN DIAGRAM to each student.

2. Students can use the Venn diagram to compare and contrast two characters from the same story or from different stories. Or they can compare themselves to a character in a story they have read.

3. Instruct students to write the names of the two characters they're comparing in the rectangles above the two figures.

4. Invite students to use colored pencils or markers to add details to the figures.

5. In the circle next to each figure, have students write words and phrases that describe the unique qualities of that character.

6. Have students write traits the two characters share in the area where the circles overlap.

Cross-Curriculum

Students can use the graphic organizer to examine the similarities and differences between two explorers, inventors, artists, or authors.

Teacher Tip

Use this graphic organizer as a "getting to know you" activity at the beginning of the year. Pair up students and have them discuss interests and hobbies they share and their likes and dislikes. Have students each decorate a figure to look like themselves and enter the information in the Venn diagram. Display the completed pages on a bulletin board under a banner that reads, GETTING TO KNOW YOU.

Name _____

Date _____

Character Counts Venn Diagram

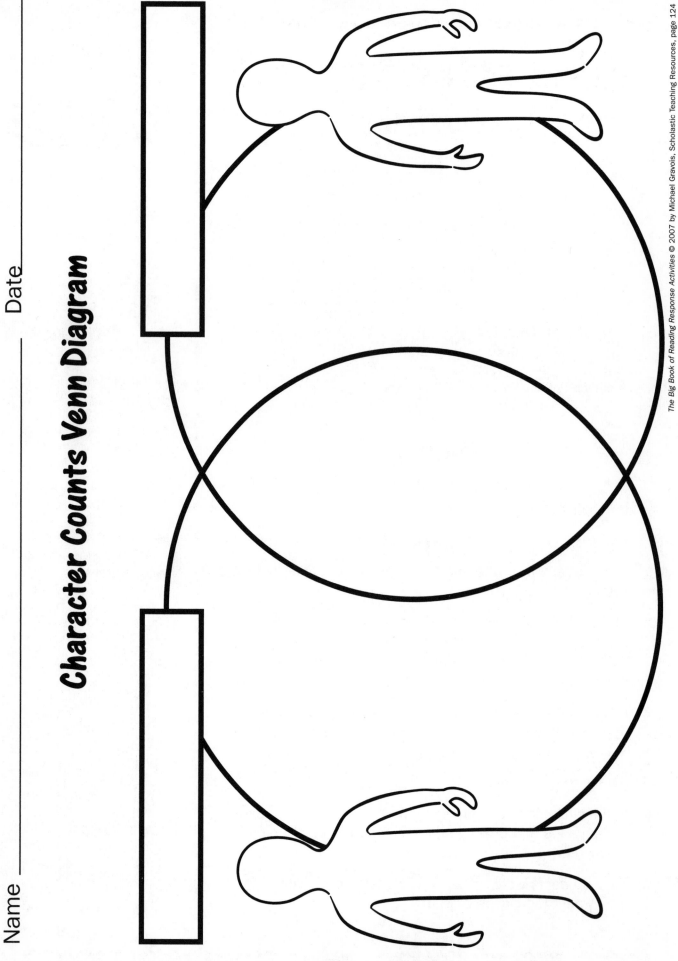

Character Coat of Arms

Materials

- COAT OF ARMS template (page 126)
- colored pencils or markers
- scissors
- tape

Cross-Curriculum

Have students create an "All About Me" coat of arms with icons representing their interests, families, and accomplishments.

Purpose

Students demonstrate knowledge of a character's traits, development, and significance in a story.

Directions

1. Explain to the class the significance of a family coat of arms, mentioning that the objects on it reflect important aspects of a family's history. Show examples if possible.

2. Give each student a copy of the COAT OF ARMS template.

3. In the center box on the coat of arms, have students write the name of a character from a book they've read.

4. In each of the quadrants, have students draw a picture that represents an important aspect of the character. Pictures can represent character traits, events from the book, important objects associated with the character, and so on.

5. Have students cut out their coat of arms, keeping the tabs attached, and fold back the tabs behind the shield.

6. Collect the projects. Tape the tabs so that when you attach the coat of arms to the bulletin board, they curve outward, creating a 3-D effect.

Teacher Tip

Add a writing component to this activity by asking students to create a scroll out of white construction paper that includes a descriptive sentence about each of the illustrations on the coat of arms. Show students how to curl the top and bottom of the construction paper forward and backward respectively, so that it looks like a scroll. Have them tape the curled paper into place. Add the scrolls next to the coats of arms on the bulletin board.

Name _____ Date _____

Coat of Arms Template

tab

tab

A Change in Character

Cause and Effect
- Graphic Organizer -
Fiction

Materials

- A CHANGE IN CHARACTER graphic organizer (page 128)
- colored pencils or markers

Purpose

Students examine the ways in which a character changes and grows over the course of a story.

Directions

1. Give each student a copy of the A CHANGE IN CHARACTER graphic organizer.

2. Instruct students to write the name of a character in the box at the top of the page.

3. Have students describe how the character feels or acts at the beginning of the story. Tell them to write their description in the book on the left side of the graphic organizer.

4. In the arrow at the center of the organizer, instruct students to write a description of an event that caused the character to change.

5. In the book on the right side of the organizer, have students write about how the character feels or acts *after* the event.

Teacher Tip

Connect this activity to the lives of your students. Ask them to name something that has happened in their lives and how their feelings or actions changed because of it. Could it be the birth of a baby sister? Moving to a new city? Taking a trip? Trying a new food?

Name _____

Date _____

A Change in Character

character's name: _____

Before

How does the character feel or act at the beginning of the story?

Cause

What causes the character to change?

After

How does the character feel or act at the end of the story?

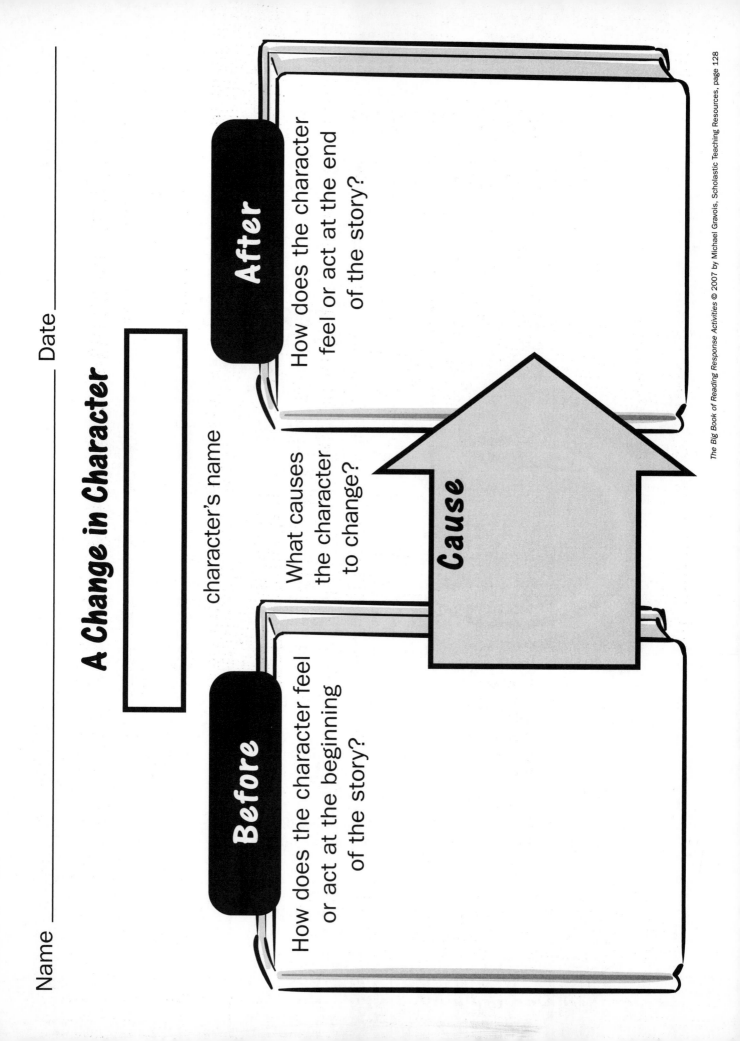

Character Flip-Flop Books

Materials

- FLIP-FLOP template (page 131)
- glue sticks or spray glue
- white construction paper
- scissors
- colored pencils or markers
- nontoxic, washable ink pads

Purpose

Students analyze the ways in which events in a story impact a character's development.

Directions

1. Give each student a copy of the FLIP-FLOP template.

2. Have students use glue sticks to glue the templates to white construction paper. This prevents the ink from showing through and gives the project a more finished look.

3. Show students how to cut each of the dotted lines on their templates, making sure to stop where the dotted line meets the solid line.

Teacher Tip

Before conducting this activity, lead a class discussion about character development. Begin by connecting this concept to the students' lives. Ask students to name ways they've grown in the past year—physically, intellectually, emotionally, morally, and socially. Then discuss ways in which a fictional character has grown over the course of a story. Ask students whether any of them have grown in similar ways. Tracking the development of a fictional character helps students better understand their own growth and maturation.

4. Ask students to fold down the flaps so that the lines are on the inside of the fold.

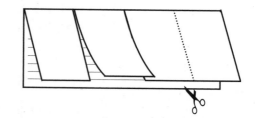

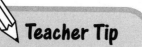

Teacher Tip

A thumbnail sketch is a small, rough sketch that helps an artist quickly explore possible layouts for a drawing they will be creating. Encourage your students to draw a thumbnail sketch for each of the illustrations on their flip-flop book. This will help them figure out the orientation and proper location of the thumbprint for each flap.

5. Instruct students to choose four events that play a major role in the development of a character from a book they've read. Have students write a few descriptive sentences about each event under the flaps of their flip-flop book, from left to right, starting with the first event and ending with the fourth event.

6. On the front of each panel, instruct students to use an ink pad to make a thumbprint. Invite them to use colored pencils or markers to make the thumbprints into cartoons of the character experiencing the events. See the example on page 129.

7. Display the completed flip-flop books on a bulletin board under a banner that reads CHARACTER DEVELOPMENT AT OUR FINGERTIPS.

Problem and Solution
- Bulletin Board -
Fiction

Problem & Solution Jigsaw Puzzles

Problem
The farmer doesn't want to keep Wilbur.

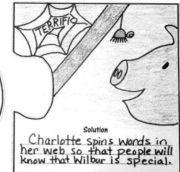

Solution
Charlotte spins words in her web so that people will know that Wilbur is special.

Teacher Tip

Use these templates to study dual concepts such as cause and effect, fact and opinion, true and false. Simply cover the "problem" and "solution" titles on each jigsaw piece before copying.

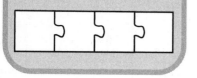

Leveling Tip

Create interior puzzle pieces by overlapping the right half of template 1 with the left half of template 2. Older students can create longer puzzle strips that focus on sequencing main events of a story.

Materials

- JIGSAW templates (pages 133–134)
- colored pencils or markers
- scissors
- tape

Purpose

Students demonstrate a knowledge of the concept of problem and solution in a literary text.

Directions

1. A good story has a problem and a solution that fit together like perfectly matched jigsaw pieces. Have students write a sentence on the lines of Jigsaw template 1 that describes the main problem of a story. Tell them to draw and color a picture of this problem in the space above the sentence.

2. Have students write a sentence on the lines of Jigsaw template 2 that describes the solution to the problem. Have them draw and color a picture of the solution.

3. Instruct students to cut out the jigsaw pieces and tape them together from behind.

4. Have them write their name and the title of the story on a strip of paper. Hang the puzzle pieces on a bulletin board with the corresponding titles above them. Add a banner that reads, PROBLEM SOLVED!

Name _____ Date _____

Jigsaw Template 1

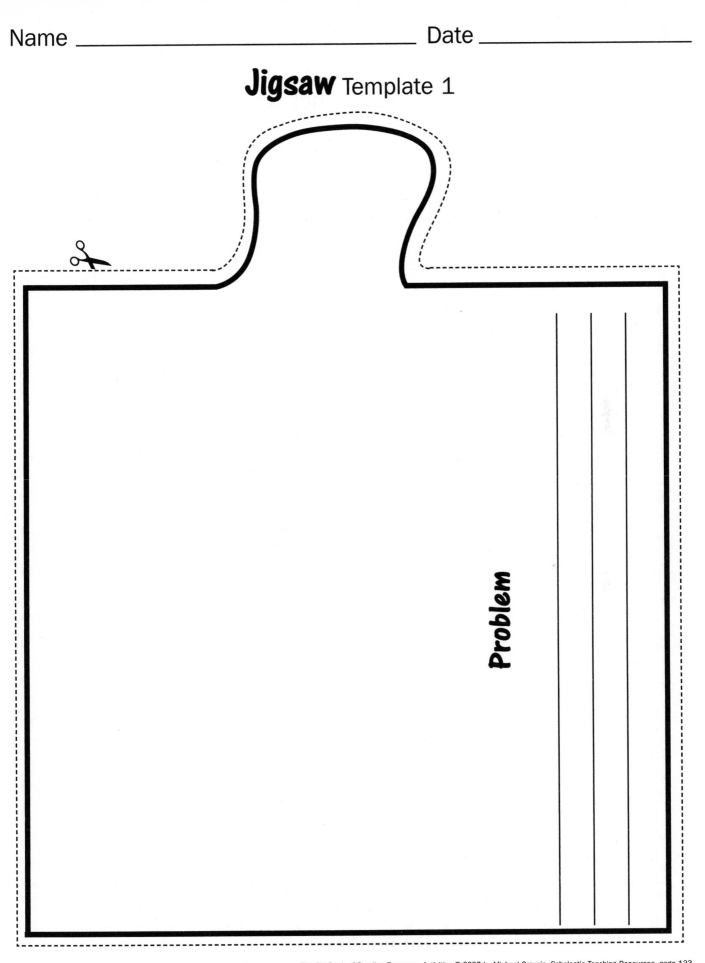

Problem

Name _____ Date _____

Jigsaw Template 2

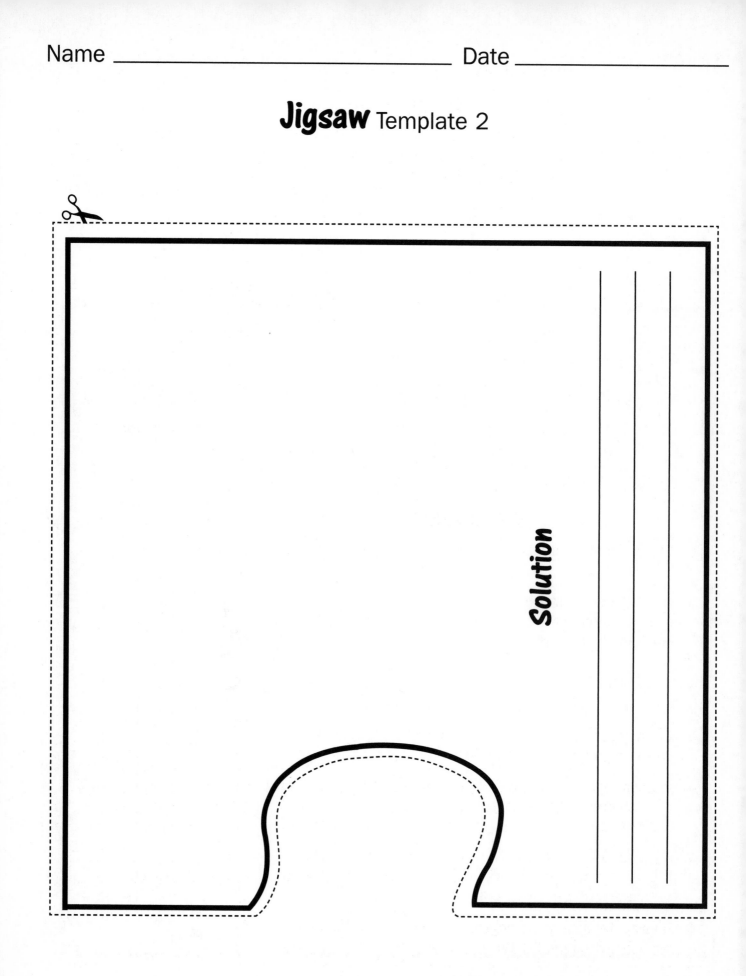

Solution

I've Got a Bone to Pick

Critiquing and Reviewing
- Bulletin Board -
Fiction/Nonfiction

Logan

Armadilly Chili by Helen Ketteman

I liked learning about the different animals in Texas and how it's nice to have friends.

Materials

- I'VE GOT A BONE TO PICK templates (pages 136–137)
- scissors
- colored pencils or markers

Purpose

Students describe things they liked and disliked about a story.

Directions

1. Give each student a copy of the two I'VE GOT A BONE TO PICK templates.

2. Have students cut out the bones on the first template—making sure to keep the bones connected—and fold it along the dotted line.

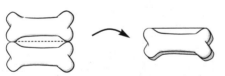

3. On the topmost bone have students write a sentence describing what they liked most about a story they read.

4. Instruct students to open the top flap. On the interior bone have students write a sentence describing something they disliked about the story or something they would change.

5. Have each student color and cut out the dog on template 2 and write their name on the dog's collar. Have them write the story's title and author on the side of the dog.

6. Display the bones and dogs on a bulletin board under a banner that reads, I'VE GOT A BONE TO PICK.

Teacher Tip

If you would like students to have more writing space, enlarge the bone when you copy it. Or you could staple a couple of completed bones together to create a shape book with more pages.

Name _____ Date _____

I've Got a Bone to Pick Template 1

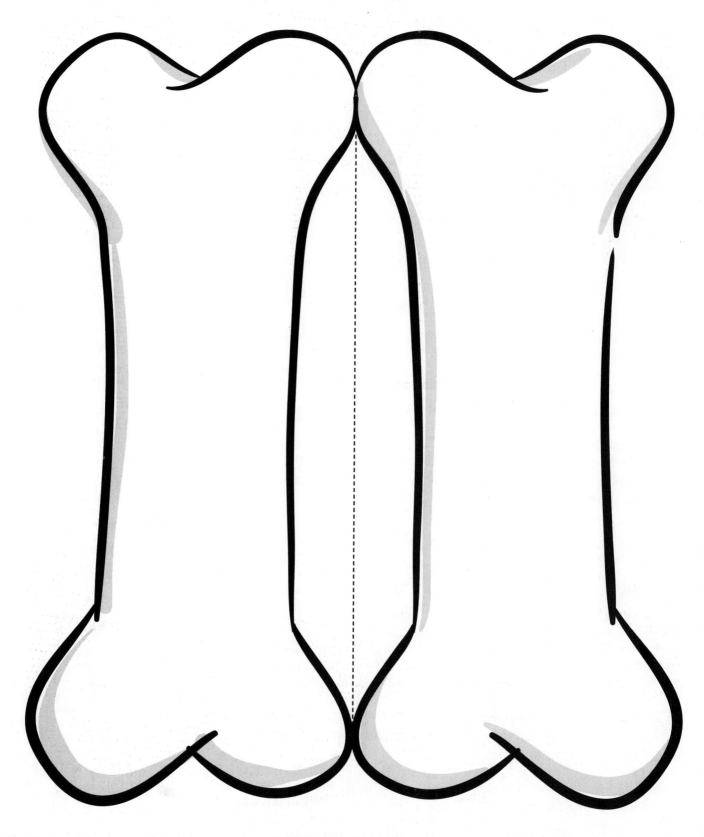

I've Got a Bone to Pick Template 2

"Who Am I?" Headbands

Purpose

Students ask yes or no questions to try to guess the names of characters from stories they read.

Directions

1. Before conducting this activity with the class, place index cards vertically in front of you. At the top of the cards, write the names of major characters from books the class has read throughout the year.

2. Cut lengths of newsprint that measure 5 by 24 inches, and give one to each student.

3. Ask students to fold the strip in half lengthwise.

4. Wrap the strips around students' heads with the folded edge at the bottom. Tape the strip at the back so it becomes a crown.

5. Place an index card in the fold above each student's forehead so the character's name faces forward. Do not let the students see their own card.

Teacher Tip

This is a great end-of-the-year activity that encourages the class to revisit the various characters and books they enjoyed throughout the year.

6. One by one, invite students to stand in front of the class and have them try to guess the character on their headband by asking yes or no questions, such as "Am I an animal?" or "Am I a real person?"

7. See who can guess his or her character in the fewest guesses.

Alternate Activity

1. You can also make this a team game. Divide the class into two teams—Team A and Team B.

2. Instruct each team to write the names of characters on index cards, which the opposing team will try to guess.

3. Members from Team A will place their cards in the head-bands of Team B members. Team B will do the same for Team A.

4. Invite one person from Team A to the front of the class. This student has one minute to ask as many yes or no questions and make as many guesses as possible. Team A scores one point if the student guesses the character correctly.

5. Alternate between the two teams until everyone has had a chance to ask questions. The team with the most points wins.

Cross-Curriculum

Don't limit yourself to the names of people. Play "Who Am I?" "Where Am I?" or "What Am I?" Think of ways this fun, out-of-your-seats activity can be used across the curriculum. Try playing the game using the names of animals, careers, cities, book titles, countries, body parts, vegetables, simple machines, or things found in space.

Story Quilts

Materials

- STORY QUILT template (page 141)
- colored pencils or markers
- scissors
- tape

Purpose

Students demonstrate a knowledge of basic story elements.

Directions

1. Show students examples of fabrics that feature repetitive designs to give them an idea for the "swatches" of fabric they will be creating for their story quilts.

2. Give each student a copy of the STORY QUILT template.

3. In the center of the quilt, have students use creative lettering to write the book's title, the author's name, and their own name.

4. In the eight outer sections around the center square, instruct students to create designs in repetitive patterns that illustrate aspects of the story. (For example, if a student were reporting on *Charlotte's Web*, one swatch could feature spider webs, another could feature blue ribbons, and another could feature farm animals.)

5. On the back of the quilt, encourage students to write a sentence about each of the swatches, describing each design's significance.

6. When they are done, ask students to cut out the quilt pattern.

7. Lay the patterns next to each other, facedown. Tape them together to form a large quilt.

8. Display the quilt in the hall or on a classroom wall.

Teacher Tip

Creating story quilts is a great end-of-the-year activity. Ask each student to create a quilt block for a different story the class read throughout the year.

Cross-Curriculum

Quilting activities help students focus on the details of a topic. For example, have students create a class quilt that illustrates sea life, types of weather, or habitats.

Story Quilt Template

Fact Frames

Materials

- 9- by 12-inch construction paper
- rulers
- scissors
- colored pencils or markers
- glue sticks

Purpose

Students summarize and paraphrase information gathered from a nonfiction text.

Directions

1. Give each student two pieces of 9- by 12-inch construction paper.

2. Tell them to cut a 3-inch strip off each piece of paper, as shown, leaving two 9-inch squares. Then have students cut one inch off two sides of one square, leaving an 8-inch square.

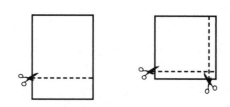

3. Ask students to fold the 8-inch square in half diagonally two times; and then have them unfold the last fold, so the square is still folded in half.

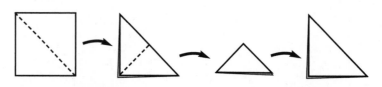

4. Show students how to carefully cut along the fold line toward the outside corner, stopping one inch before reaching the corner.

5. Tell students to unfold the square and refold along the cut they just made. They should repeat step 4, cutting along the remaining fold. When they unfold the square the cuts form an X in the middle of the square.

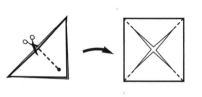

6. Ask students to fold open the four triangular flaps back and forth. Have them cut 1 inch off the points of each flap, leaving a window in the center of the square, as shown at right.

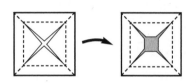

7. Instruct students to rub a glue stick around the outer edges of the 8-inch square and glue it in the center of the 9-inch square. Have them fold down the flaps.

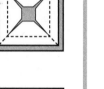

8. Ask students to pick a nonfiction topic to research (such as a famous person or an animal habitat). Tell them to draw an icon in the window that represents the main idea of their topic. (You might allow students to print a small picture from the Internet and glue it in the window.)

9. On the top of each of the four flaps, students should write the title of a category related to their topic. For example, if they were reporting on animals in the rain forest, the four flaps could read "food," "appearance," "habitat," and "life span."

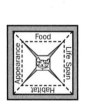

10. Beneath each flap, tell students to write facts that they gathered about the topic.

11. Invite students to decorate the outer edges of their fact frames.

Teacher Tip

Hang the fact frames side by side on a bulletin board to form a large quilt of the students' work. Add a banner that reads, FACT FRAMES.

Rising and Falling Action

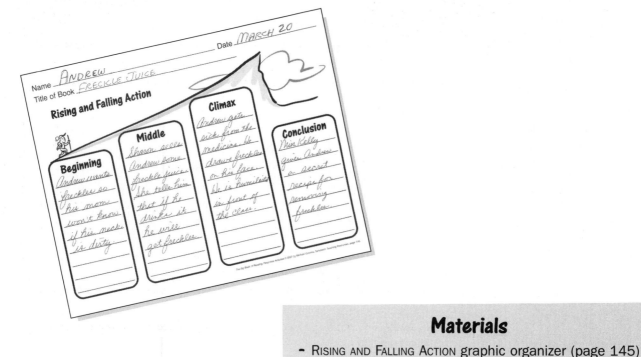

Materials

- RISING AND FALLING ACTION graphic organizer (page 145)

Purpose

Students analyze the way in which a story builds toward a climax and resolution.

Directions

1. Discuss with the class the idea of rising and falling action—how a story builds over time, leading to a climax and then quickly concluding. Use a familiar story, such as *Cinderella*, to point out these elements.

2. Give each student a copy of the RISING AND FALLING ACTION graphic organizer.

3. Ask students to write sentences that describe the beginning, middle, climax, and conclusion of a story they've read.

Name _____

Date _____

Book Title _____

Rising and Falling Action

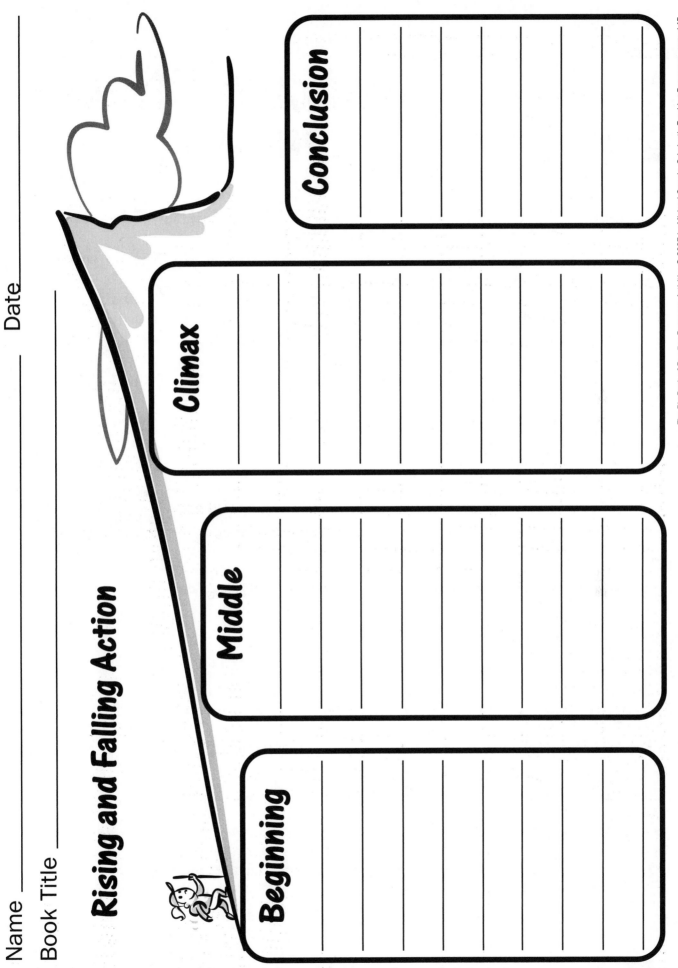

Beginning

Middle

Climax

Conclusion

The Big Book of Reading Response Activities © 2007 by Michael Gravois, Scholastic Teaching Resources, page 145

Nonfiction Class Murals

Materials

- white bulletin board paper
- scissors
- colored pencils or markers
- construction paper
- index cards
- glue

Teacher Tip

Class murals are great fun to create because they make the classroom come alive with the curriculum being studied. They also give students a sense of ownership of the classroom.

Purpose

Students create a large mural featuring elements found in a nonfiction setting.

Directions

1. Start by cutting a sheet of white bulletin board paper to mural size—the length of a wall in the hall or inside your classroom.

2. Lay the paper on the floor and have students create a background related to a nonfiction book you are reading (for example, the ocean floor, a distant planet, or the rain forest). You might assign small sections to each student so that everyone has his or her own space.

3. After the background is drawn, have students brainstorm a list of things that are related to the topic. If the topic is the deserts of America, for example, your list might include rattlesnakes, horned toads, scorpions, tumbleweeds, and prickly pears.

4. Have each student choose a different item from the list to research. (Consider allowing no more than two students to select the same item, to provide more visual variety in the mural.)

5. After students complete their research, have them draw on a sheet of construction paper a picture of the item they studied. (Urge students to examine the placement of the item in the mural to help them determine its size.) To make the mural three-dimensional, students can add extra elements to their illustrations. For example, they can create tarantulas with pipe-cleaner legs, comets with crepe-paper tails, and fish with fins that stick out.

6. On an index card, have students write a paragraph that includes four or five key facts about the item they researched.

7. Invite students each to give a short oral report on their findings and then attach the object and index card to the mural.

8. Display the mural in the hall or across a wall in the classroom.

Cross-Curriculum

This is a perfect project for your school's art teacher to lead, and it will help students understand the way all subjects are integrated.

Story Necklaces

Teacher Tip

Help students become confident public speakers by introducing public speaking in an easy, non-threatening way. The more often you have students speak in front of the class, the more comfortable they will become.

Teacher Tip

Story necklaces can be used to highlight other reading skills and story elements. Students can create character necklaces that feature the cast of characters from the story, or they can create problem-and-solution necklaces that emphasize the obstacles in the story that the main character must overcome.

Materials

- hole punch
- index cards
- colored pencils or markers
- yarn
- scissors

Purpose

Students retell a story, using illustrations as prompts to help them describe its beginning, middle, and end.

Directions

1. Give each student three index cards.

2. On the blank side of the cards, have students draw pictures that represent the beginning, the middle, and the end of a story.

3. As students finish each drawing, have them punch a hole in the top center of the card. (The orientation of the picture will determine whether the card is horizontal or vertical.)

4. Have students thread a length of yarn through the holes so the cards fall in sequential order from left to right.

5. Tie the yarn loosely around each child's neck.

6. Invite students to the front of the class so they can retell the story in their own words, using the illustrations on their story necklaces as prompts.

Story Wheels

Story Elements
- Activity -
Fiction

Materials

- STORY WHEEL template (page 150)
- scissors
- colored pencils or markers

Purpose

Students create a wheel to display basic story elements.

Directions

1. Pass out a copy of the STORY WHEEL template to each student.

2. Instruct students to write their name in the center oval.

3. In the top segment, have students write the title of the book and the author's name.

4. In the other segments, have students draw a picture of the protagonist, the main setting, and the problem and solution of the story.

5. Instruct students to cut out the story wheels.

6. Display the projects on a bulletin board under a banner that reads, STORY WHEELS of _____, filling in the title of the story.

Teacher Tip

If you'd like students to have more drawing or writing space, have them create a large story wheel by tracing the outline of a large bowl onto a sheet of white bulletin board paper.

Name _____ Date _____

Story Wheel Template

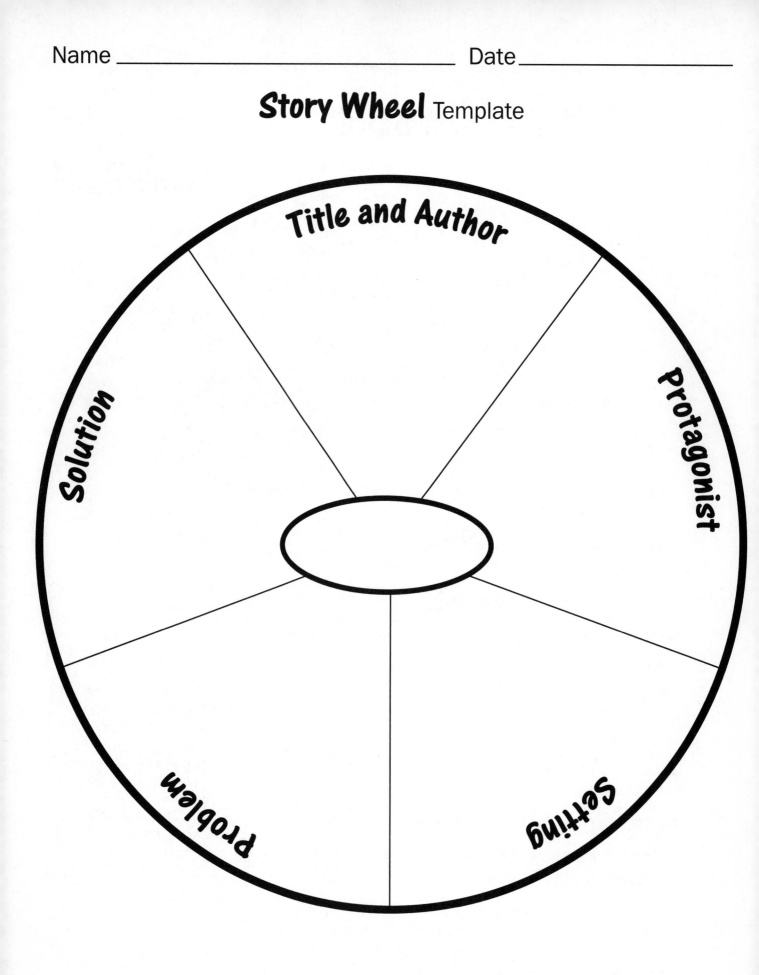

Title and Author

Protagonist

Solution

Setting

Problem

Story Towers

Materials

- 4- by 6-inch index cards
- colored pencils or markers
- rulers
- scissors

Purpose

Students show an understanding of how a story's plot is made up of a series of related events.

Directions

1. In advance, place two marks at the top of each index card, one inch from the left side and one inch from the right side. Then, do the same thing at the bottom of the card.

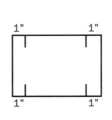

2. Discuss with students the idea that main events are the building blocks of a story's plot. If one event is missing, the plot's structure weakens. Give examples from a story you've read in class.

3. After reading a book (or while you're reading it), make a list of the important events.

4. Give each student an index card and assign each student a different event.

5. On the blank side of the card, instruct students to draw a picture of their assigned event. On the lined side, have them write a paragraph describing the event.

6. Show students how to cut the card at the tick marks, one-half inch toward the center of the cards.

7. Invite students to create a story tower by locking the cards together. The cards for the first two scenes should be at the bottom, the third and fourth scenes on top of those, and so on.

Cross-Curriculum

Have students research the history and architecture of famous towers around the world. Have them draw a picture of the tower on one side of the card and write about its history on the other side. Some famous towers include the Eiffel Tower, the Seattle Space Needle, the Leaning Tower of Pisa, the Sears Tower in Chicago, and the Tower of London.

Art Appreciation
- Activity -
Fiction

Caldecott Posters

Materials

- copies of Caldecott Medal–winning books
- posterboard
- art supplies

Purpose

Students create a poster for a story they've read, using the artistic style of the book's illustrator.

Directions

1. Gather a few dozen copies of Caldecott Medal–winning books. A list of the award winners can be found on page 158.

2. Tell the class the Caldecott Medal is given each year to the illustrator of the most distinguished American children's picture book.

3. Show students examples of different artistic styles used in picture books—collage, watercolor, pen and ink, charcoal, acrylic, woodcut, and so on.

4. Place the books on a table and invite students to each select a book to read.

5. Give each student a sheet of posterboard and ask them to create a poster for the book they read, using the same artistic style as the book. Tell students not to simply copy a picture from the book but to create one in the style of the artist. Remind students to include the title of the book and the names of the author and illustrator on their poster. (You might ask your school's art teacher to lead this activity.)

6. After students have finished their posters, ask them to give a short book talk about the book they read and the art style they used.

Book Talk

"Illustration in children's picture books can be appreciated both for its ability to help tell the story (cognitive value) and for its value as art (aesthetic value). It takes only a moment to call to your students' attention particularly striking and unusual illustrations. By doing so, you show them that you value art. You can also discuss the artist's style, the medium used, the palette, and how the artist's style compares to others."

—Carol Lynch-Brown and Carl M. Tomlinson (1993)

Caldecott Medal Winners

Book Reports
- Activity -
Fiction

Materials

- copies of Caldecott Medal–winning books
- CALDECOTT MEDAL BOOK REPORT templates (pages 155–157)
- scissors
- colored pencils or markers
- hole punch
- brass paper fasteners

Purpose

Students demonstrate a knowledge of story structure, character development, setting, and other story elements as they create a report on an award-winning book.

Directions

1. Gather copies of Caldecott Medal–winning books. A list of the award winners can be found on page 158.

2. Let each student choose a book about which they will write a book report.

3. Make copies of the CALDECOTT MEDAL BOOK REPORT templates 1–3. (Decide the types of things on which you want the students to report, in order to determine the number of copies you'll need to make of each interior template page. A suggested list of topics can be found on page 154.)

4. Tell students to use template 1 for the report cover. Have them write their name, the title of the book they read, the author, and the illustrator.

5. Tell students to use templates 2 and 3 for the interior pages of the report. Create a topic sheet that list the things on which you want students to report on these pages.

6. After students have finished creating the cover and pages, assist them as they cut out the pages, put them in order, punch holes on the two asterisks, and fasten them together with two brass paper fasteners.

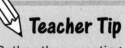

Teacher Tip

Rather than creating a separate topic sheet that lists what you want students to include on each interior page, write the topic at the top of the template page before making copies. Students can complete individual pages in class or for homework.

Suggested Topics

Here is a list of ideas that students can write about and illustrate on the interior pages of their book report. Choose the ones that work best for you and type up a topic sheet for students to use.

- On template 2, write a summary of the story.

- On template 3, draw a picture of the main character. On the lines, write five adjectives that describe this character.

- On template 3, draw a picture of the setting. On the lines, write five adjectives that describe the setting.

- On template 2, write five new words you learned in the story. Include the definitions next to each word.

- On template 3, draw a picture of your favorite scene. Write a sentence describing what's happening.

- On template 3, draw a picture of the story's main problem. Write a sentence describing the problem.

- On template 3, draw a picture of the solution to the problem. Write a sentence describing the solution.

- On template 2, write a paragraph describing why you think this book won the Caldecott Medal. What made it so outstanding?

- On template 2, write a paragraph about the author and illustrator of the book. Use the Internet and other books they may have written or illustrated to learn more about them.

- On template 2, write a paragraph about the history of the Caldecott Medal.

- On template 2, write a review of the book. Did you like it? Why? Why not?

Teacher Tip

Help students understand your expectations by creating a rubric that shows things on which they'll be evaluated—such as handwriting, spelling, punctuation, grammar, and organization.

Name _____ Date _____

Caldecott Medal Book Report Template 1

Use this for the cover of your report.

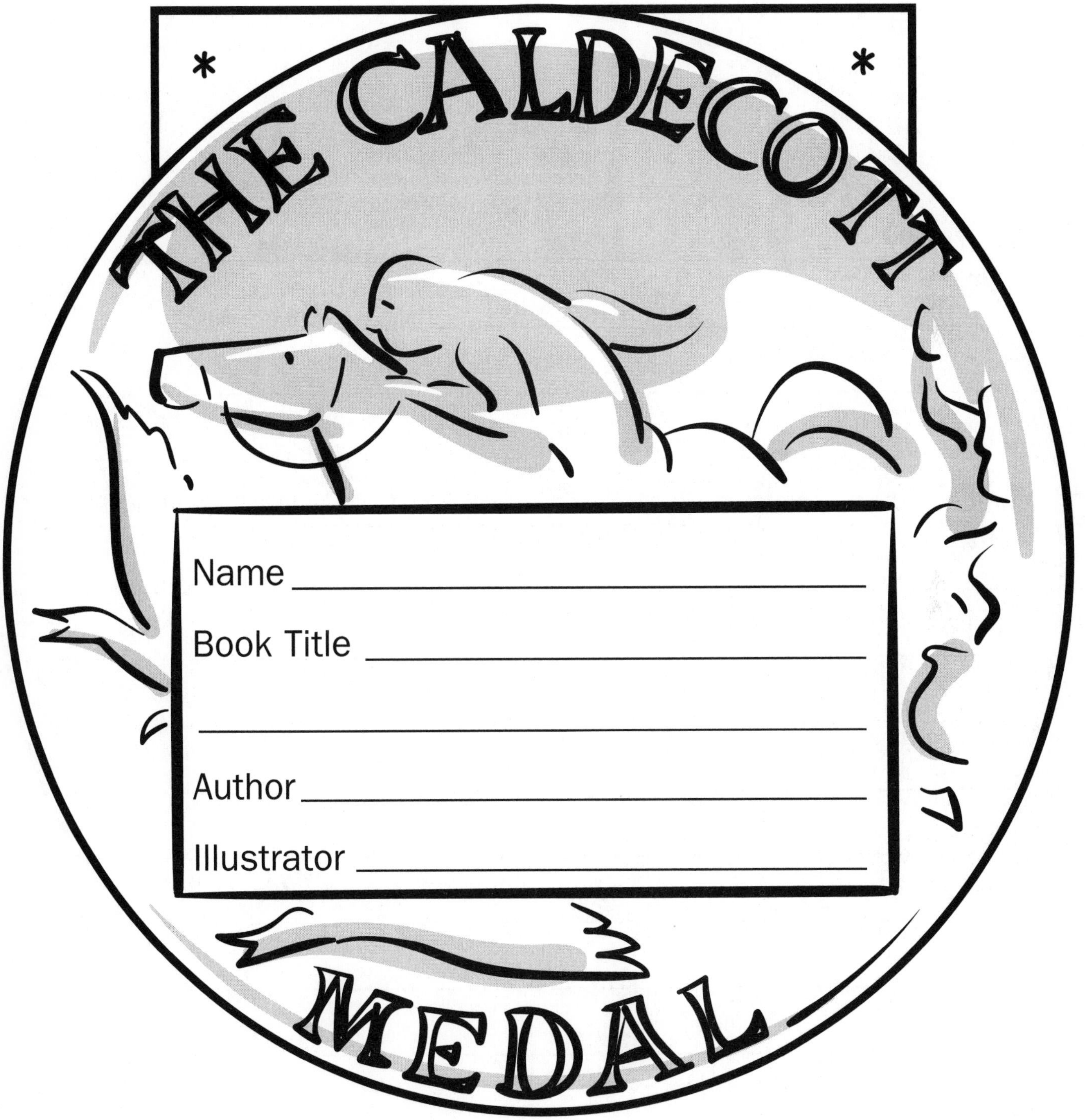

THE CALDECOTT

*   *

MEDAL

Name _____

Book Title _____

_____

Author _____

Illustrator _____

Name _____ Date _____

Caldecott Medal Book Report Template 2

Use this as a writing template.

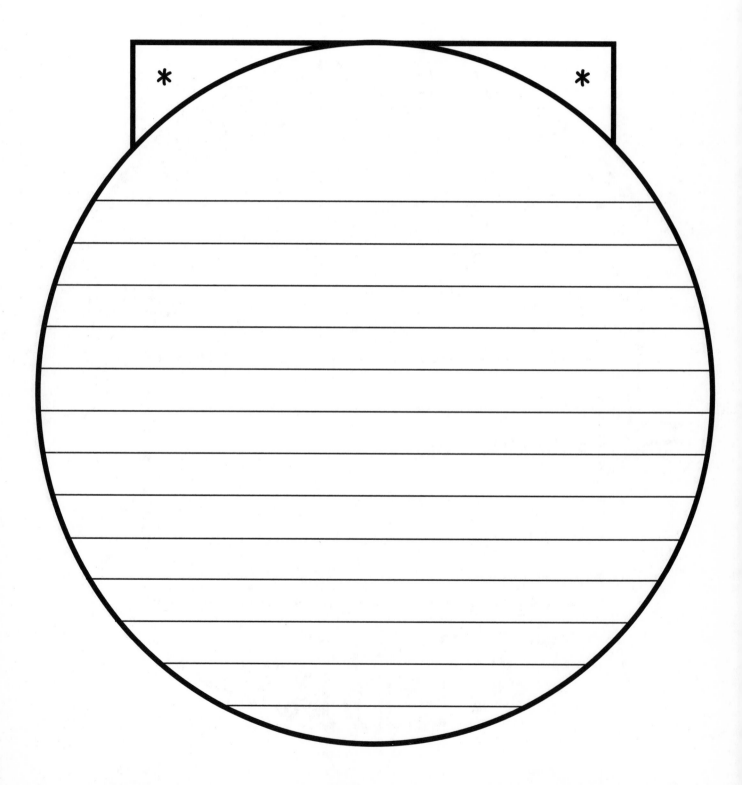

Name _____ Date _____

Caldecott Medal Book Report Template 3
Use this as a drawing template.

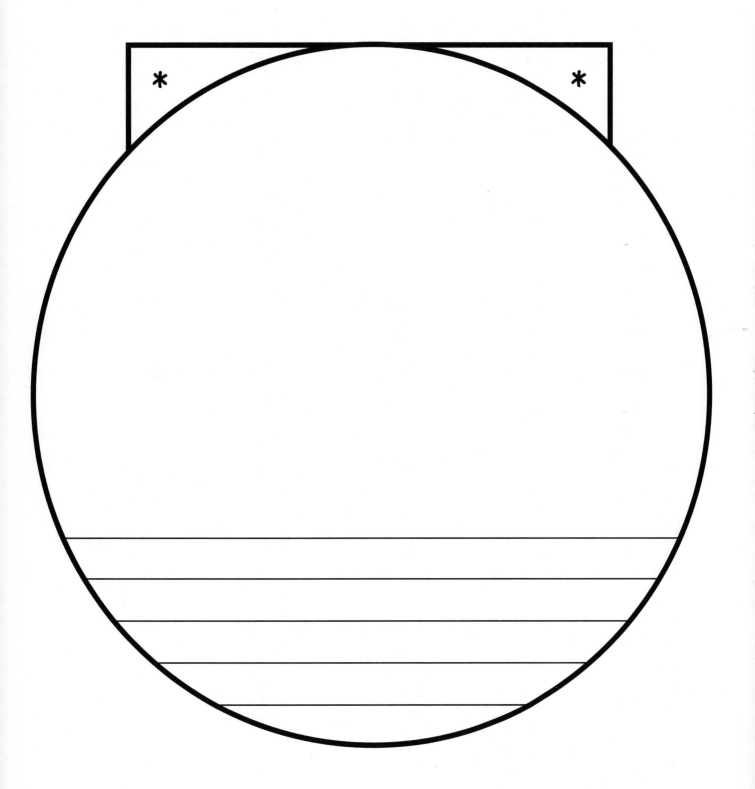

Caldecott Medal Winners

2007
David Wiesner
Flotsam

2006
Chris Raschka
*The Hello,
Goodbye Window*

2005
Kevin Henkes
*Kitten's First
Full Moon*

2004
Mordicai Gerstein
*The Man Who
Walked Between
the Towers*

2003
Eric Rohmann
My Friend Rabbit

2002
David Wiesner
The Three Pigs

2001
David Small
*So You Want to Be
President?*

2000
Simms Taback
*Joseph Had a
Little Overcoat*

1999
Mary Azarian
Snowflake Bentley

1998
Paul O. Zelinsky
Rapunzel

1997
David Wisniewski
Golem

1996
Peggy Rathmann
*Officer Buckle
and Gloria*

1995
David Diaz
Smoky Night

1994
Allen Say
*Grandfather's
Journey*

1993
Emily Arnold
*Mirette on the
High Wire*

1992
David Wiesner
Tuesday

1991
David Macaulay
Black and White

1990
Ed Young
*Lon Po Po:
A Red-Riding Hood
Story From China*

1989
Stephen Gammell
*Song and
Dance Man*

1988
John Schoenherr
Owl Moon

1987
Richard Egielski
Hey, Al

1986
Chris Van Allsburg
The Polar Express

1985
Trina Schart Hyman
*Saint George
and the Dragon*

1984
Alice and Martin
Provensen
*The Glorious Flight:
Across the Channel
With Louis Bleriot*

1983
Marcia Brown
Shadow

1982
Chris Van Allsburg
Jumanji

1981
Arnold Lobel
Fables

1980
Barbara Cooney
Ox-Cart Man

1979
Paul Goble
*The Girl Who
Loved Wild Horses*

1978
Peter Spier
Noah's Ark

1977
Leo and
Diane Dillon
*Ashanti to Zulu:
African Traditions*

1976
Leo and
Diane Dillon
*Why Mosquitoes
Buzz in
People's Ears*

1975
Gerald McDermott
Arrow to the Sun

1974
Margot Zemach
Duffy and the Devil

1973
Blair Lent
*The Funny
Little Woman*

1972
Nonny Hogrogian
One Fine Day

1971
Gail E. Haley
A Story, a Story

1970
William Steig
*Sylvester and the
Magic Pebble*

1969
Uri Shulevitz
*The Fool of the
World and the
Flying Ship*

1968
Ed Emberley
Drummer Hoff

1967
Evaline Ness
*Sam, Bangs
and Moonshine*

1966
Nonny Hogrogian
*Always Room
for One More*

1965
Beni Montresor
*May I Bring
a Friend?*

1964
Maurice Sendak
*Where the
Wild Things Are*

1963
Ezra Jack Keats
The Snowy Day

1962
Marcia Brown
Once a Mouse

1961
Nicolas Sidjakov
*Baboushka and
the Three Kings*

1960
Marie Hall Ets
*Nine Days to
Christmas*

1959
Barbara Cooney
*Chanticleer
and the Fox*

1958
Robert McCloskey
Time of Wonder

1957
Marc Simont
A Tree Is Nice

1956
Feodor Rojankovsky
Frog Went A-Courtin'

1955
Marcia Brown
*Cinderella, or the
Little Glass Slipper*

1954
Ludwig Bemelmans
Madeline's Rescue

1953
Lynd Ward
The Biggest Bear

1952
Nicolas Mordvinoff
Finders Keepers

1951
Katherine Milhous
The Egg Tree

1950
Leo Politi
*Song of the
Swallows*

1949
Berta and
Elmer Hader
The Big Snow

1948
Roger Duvoisin
*White Snow,
Bright Snow*

1947
Leonard Weisgard
The Little Island

1946
Maude and
Miska Petersham
The Rooster Crows

1945
Elizabeth
Orton Jones
Prayer for a Child

1944
Louis Slobodkin
Many Moons

1943
Virginia Lee Burton
The Little House

1942
Robert McCloskey
*Make Way
for Ducklings*

1941
Robert Lawson
*They Were
Strong and Good*

1940
Ingri and Edgar
Parin d'Aulaire
Abraham Lincoln

1939
Thomas Handforth
Mei Li

1938
Dorothy P. Lathrop
*Animals of
the Bible,
A Picture Book*

Reading Garden

Book Reports
- Bulletin Board -
Fiction

Hatchet
by Gary
Paulsen

Report by
Mary

Materials

- ruffled coffee filters
- colored pencils
- light green construction paper
- scissors
- stapler

Purpose

Students demonstrate a knowledge of a story's setting.

Directions

1. Pass out a ruffled coffee filter to each student.

2. In the center circle of the filter, have students use colored pencils to draw a picture of their favorite scene from a book they've read.

3. Pass out green construction paper to students and instruct them to cut out two large leaves and a stem.

4. Have students write the title of the book and the author's name in one leaf and their name in the other leaf.

5. Staple the leaves and stem to a bulletin board. Staple the coffee filters to the top of the stems to create a garden of books.

6. Display a banner at the top of the bulletin board that reads, TAKE A WALK THROUGH OUR READING GARDEN!

Leveling Tip

For a more detailed, written book report, students can cut a dirt mound out of tan construction paper that can be stapled at the bottom of each stem. Have students write their report on the tan paper.

Cross-Curriculum

Have students use these flowers to report on books about plant life.

Bibliography

Sources
for
Quotations

Beers, K. (2003). *When kids can't read what teachers can do.* Portsmouth, NH: Heinemann.

Keenan, G. F. (1993). "American additions." *New Oxford Review*, 15, 23.

Lynch-Brown, C. and Tomlinson, C. (1993). *Essentials of children's literature.* Boston: Allyn and Bacon.

Ogle, D. (1986). "K-W-L: A teaching model that develops active reading of expository text." *The Reading Teacher*, 39, 564–570.

Robb, L. (1996). "Reading clinic: Use predictions to help kids think deeply about books." *Instructor Magazine*, 106, 61–63.

Smith, C. B. (1991). "The role of different literary genres." *The Reading Teacher*, 44(6), 440–441.